Composition for Personal Growth:

Values Clarification through Writing

Composition for Personal Growth:
Values Clarification through Writing

SIDNEY B. SIMON, Ed.D.
CENTER FOR HUMANISTIC EDUCATION
UNIVERSITY OF MASSACHUSETTS, AMHERST

ROBERT C. HAWLEY, Ed.D.
DIRECTOR, EDUCATION RESEARCH ASSOCIATES
AMHERST, MASSACHUSETTS

DAVID D. BRITTON, Ed.D.
DIRECTOR, ALTERNATIVE SCHOOL PROJECT
HINESBURG, VERMONT

HART PUBLISHING COMPANY, INC.
NEW YORK CITY, NEW YORK

COPYRIGHT © 1973
HART PUBLISHING COMPANY, INC., NEW YORK, N.Y. 10003
ISBN NO. 08055-1108-3 (PAPERBACK 08055-0135-5)
LIBRARY OF CONGRESS CATALOG CARD NO. 72-96678

NO PART OF THIS BOOK MAY BE REPRODUCED OR USED
IN ANY FORM WITHOUT THE EXPRESS PERMISSION OF
THE PUBLISHER IN WRITING.

MANUFACTURED IN THE UNITED STATES OF AMERICA.

Table of Contents

6		Preface
11	Chapter 1	Composition
23	Chapter 2	Identity
63	Chapter 3	Interpersonal Relations
69	Chapter 4	Values into Action
75	Chapter 5	Personal Growth
81	Chapter 6	Implementing the "Composition for Personal Growth" Approach
105	Chapter 7	General Techniques and Activities
159	Chapter 8	Ongoing Activities
167	Chapter 9	Personal-Growth Activities for Teachers
173		Suggested Readings
179		Index

Preface

Composition for Personal Growth is a program for teaching composition to students in grades seven through twelve. Through guided activities and a wide range of written assignments, this approach attempts to promote the student's awareness of self, his ability to relate positively to others, and his ability to translate his values into meaningful actions.

Composition for Personal Growth is not in itself a complete English curriculum. It is expected that teachers who use *Composition for Personal Growth* will also include in their programs the reading of various kinds of literature, as well as other writing activities. "Creative" writing—i.e. inventing stories, plays, poems—is not included in this program per se simply because it is a somewhat different, though closely related, activity. The authors feel that stories, poems, and plays—or fragments thereof—are appropriate responses to many of the activities included here, but that the formal study of these forms lies outside the scope of this program. Similarly, questions of mechanical correctness and rhetorical effectiveness are omitted from this volume. In determining how and when to deal with these issues, the teacher should be guided by the felt needs of the students.

Although *Composition for Personal Growth* was initially designed for use in English classes, the program has been used successfully by teachers in drug education programs, by group counselors, social studies teachers, foreign language teachers, religious educators, and by leaders in youth programs, such as Scouts and YMCA.

This program aims to achieve personal growth and increased effectiveness in verbal communication. Because the basic subject matter of the program is the developing individual himself, the activities can profitably be repeated from grade level to grade level. Such repetition is rendered even more valuable if the student keeps a record of his previous responses, and can readily see his own personal growth.

We wish to thank the many teachers and students who have cooperated in the development of this program. Their responses have been helpful in many ways.

We also wish to thank Isabel L. Hawley for her assistance in revising the manuscript and preparing it for publication.

SIDNEY B. SIMON
ROBERT C. HAWLEY
DAVID D. BRITTON

Composition for Personal Growth:

Values Clarification through Writing

1

Composition

IT STANDS silent out in the open. A very small delicate tree that looks as though you could tip it over simply by breathing on it. It is very vulnerable, for no matter which way you turn there is no protection from attackers. It's very odd compared to the others for this time of year. Instead of turning many different colors, this one particular tree is still green. What few leaves it has are still dark. It most likely was planted for decoration; it's a pity nature, which demands to be free, can be told where to grow and what space we want. It's very young when compared to the others, but yet it's been here for years, watching the world pass it by. There's no way, to me, that this tree could be happy.

The assignment: Go outside and find a tree that is in some way like yourself. Draw a picture of it, and write a description of the tree. Peter Meyer, a teacher of English at Roger Ludlowe High School in Fairfield, Connecticut, invented this activity and used it with his tenth grade work-study class. The paragraph above was the work of a girl of fifteen, perhaps the most successful of the writings produced at that time. Its implications for education in general, and for the teaching of English in particular, are far-reaching.

For Peter Meyer, composition is not an artificial exercise to be produced on demand by a student for a person (the teacher) who matters little in his life, and who is unlikely to be influenced by the composition. For Peter Meyer, composition offers the student a chance to reflect upon his experience and to clarify that experience through writing. Meyer sees the teacher as a provider of opportunities for self-discovery, in this case through writing. The vehicle for self-discovery that Meyer uses is metaphor—a powerful discovery tool—for metaphor is full of surprises, of chances to make new and unusual connections.

The young girl's description of her tree has much to say to us about the current state of education and civilization. It shouts of wasted life, speaks eloquently of the barrenness and sterility a schoolgirl experiences, and scores the erosion of human potential by days and days of forced passivity in the classroom.

Frieda Fordham, in *An Introduction to Jung's Psychology,* also likens modern man to a tree, tall in material and technological achievements, but with dangerously shallow roots in his own nature:

Since the development of applied science in the last hundred years, man's material progress has been rapid, but he has moved dangerously far from his roots in the soil [of his own nature]. The taller the tree the deeper its roots should go, but modern man has little relationship with [his own] nature, and so has become dangerously unstable and a victim of any storms that blow.[1]

Traditional schooling prunes branches and trains tender shoots toward superficial aims, all the while

---

1. Frieda Fordham, *An Introduction to Jung's Psychology,* Harmondsworth, Middlesex: Penguin Books Ltd., 1966, p. 119.

neglecting the nourishment of the roots, which, hidden and silent, lie shallow and small and struggle to support the full growth of the plant. Thus is the maturing plant robbed of the full realization of the potentialities which were promised in its seed.

The problem is massive. Our schools are vast nurseries where few trees are nourished at the root. Obviously, no single program can change the entire course of schooling. *Composition for Personal Growth* has been prepared as one small step toward the nurture of the roots. It proposes, by linking personal growth to the teaching of written composition, to inject into the traditional curriculum the vital issues of personal growth and self-awareness.

Sending messages one cares to send to a receiver one hopes to influence—that is what writing is. It does not matter whether the message is an entry in a diary, a grocery list, a love letter, a poem, or a letter of complaint. Writing is a way of extending the range of one's influence across time and space, a way of extending the power of one's voice, or the reach of one's thoughts.

The traditional composition assignment violates this concept of writing in many ways:

1. The assigned message often does not seem worth sending.

2. The receiver (teacher) may not be interested or susceptible to influence.

3. The message is generally less important than the style. To write well is the goal. (Ask a group of young people to write poems, and watch them

stiffen—"Who, *me*?" Adulation of style and the accompanying aura of perfectionism create in some students a sense of humility that borders on constriction and even paralysis.)

4. Writing is conducted in a strongly negative atmosphere. Careful reading by a teacher means extensive noting of deficiencies. (Negative focus is deeply embedded in the language patterns of composition teachers: Examine the glossary of correction symbols on the endpapers of any composition handbook. We know of one which codifies 138 different kinds of errors, and has not one abbreviation for a positive comment.)

Items one and two above represent a perversion of the intrinsic motivation for writing, and train for cynicism. Items three and four vitiate external motivators, encourage avoidance behavior, and train for impotence. The combination is enough to evoke the refrain, "It's not worth doing, and I couldn't do it anyway." A teacher using such an approach to composition could be compared to Emily Post teaching a course entitled "Dating a Mannequin."

The aim of *Composition for Personal Growth* is to alter the traditional approach to the teaching of composition in the following ways:

1. *Messages worth sending:* Messages important to the young person are ones related to such questions as: Who am I? What do I value? How am I perceived by others? How might I change?

2. *Interested receivers susceptible to influence:* The important audience to a young person is one re-

lated to his needs for identity, power, and affiliation; that is, his peers, self, parents, teachers, etc.

3. *Real-world goals:* The goal of the writer is to influence his audience, not just to write well. Ideally, of course, these goals would go hand in hand.

4. *Real-world feedback:* Good writing influences its audience in the way the writer intended. Direct responses from the audience are the primary source of feedback. A secondary source of feedback comes from sharing writing and reactions with other writers.

It should be pointed out that a competitive grading system is harmful to a writing program such as this for at least two reasons: First, when a piece of writing is to be graded, the real audience is the grade-giver, regardless of who the declared audience for the message may be. Thus, influencing one's audience means doing what gets a good grade. Second, a competitive grading system inevitably designates some students as winners and some as losers. A vast body of evidence shows that this experience is not helpful to the winners and is seriously damaging to the losers.

The personal-growth approach utilizes experiences generated in various social contests by the learners themselves. The vehicles of growth and learning are the interactions themselves. Thus, the personal-growth approach induces changes in the learning process itself by communicating a particular method of inquiry and learning. The focus is on learning how to learn, and on developing critical thinking skills through thinking critically.

16] COMPOSITION FOR PERSONAL GROWTH

Much of the class time will be spent in small-group discussions and activities initiated by suggestions from the teacher, who is then free to act as consultant to individuals and groups. Occasionally, the whole class will reconvene for discussion or for large group activities or for presentations and lecturettes by members of the small groups. The teacher may meet from time to time with each of the small groups for a special discussion or activity.

The activities in the program are designed to produce written responses which may consist of anything from one word to a complete essay. The student records his responses in a private journal. Some of these responses may be recorded by another member of the peer group in his own journal. Occasionally, a writer may want to share sections of his journal with other members of the peer group.

Although the data in journals is unorganized, it is all more or less relevant to questions such as "Who am I? How am I perceived by others? Which of my characteristics are common and which are unique? What do I value?"

From time to time, the students will engage in synthesizing activities, where they explore the contents of their journals as an archaeologist might examine the artifacts unearthed in a digging.

The journals will not be read by the teacher unless the student asks specifically for consultation. Evaluation comes from the peer group discussions, where the emphasis is on content and effectiveness. The discussion of mechanics—spelling, punctuation, capitalization—comes only when the peer group finds significant interference with the message as the result of mechanical problems.

It should be emphasized that the authors of *Composition for Personal Growth* do not consider mechanics and style irrelevant to composition. However, we do feel that these aspects of writing usually receive disproportionate attention. The attempt here is to redress the balance, putting the emphasis on getting the desired message across to the desired audience. The effectiveness of the communication is of course related to its mechanical and rhetorical qualities. Thus, the study of these technical aspects of writing comes when it is needed—when there is a problem in communication or a student-initiated desire to improve communication—rather than when the textbook schedule says it's that time. Style and mechanics seem too often to be regarded as ends in themselves, instead of as means to an end—effective communication.

Clearly, the teacher is the key to the success of this program, and there are certain things which are uniquely his responsibility.

1. In his role as group facilitator, he is responsible for moving students into groups and setting up patterns for group behavior.

2. In his role as stimulator of activity, he provides engaging material for young people to discuss and to write about.

3. He serves as an additional audience, supplementing the peer group, and can thus add an additional perspective in offering feedback.

4. And perhaps most important, the teacher can help

to clarify problems that students encounter but cannot solve by themselves. Here the teacher can bring to bear his special knowledge of usage, transformational grammar, and rhetoric.

In short, the teacher must have skills in group process, a knowledge of linguistics and rhetoric, and the wisdom to judge when to intervene to create new learning opportunities, and when to refrain from intervention because his presence would inhibit learning.

The word *composition* today generally connotes that thing, often referred to as "the weekly composition," to be handed in on Monday, folded along the vertical axis, with the student's name and the date neatly placed in the upper right-hand corner. If, however, we go back to the meaning of the word *compose*, the real value of written composition becomes clear. The dictionary defines *compose* as: to form by putting together two or more things, elements or parts. It is in the act of composing—that is, putting together—the chaotic events that make up existence that we learn how to order and shape our experience, thereby learning more about our lives and about ourselves. Composition thus understood allows us to give our experience a name, and by naming it to carry out the most fundamental purpose in language—communication, the sharing of our experience with others.

But the sharing of experience is not only an end in itself; it is a valuable decision-making tool. It is through shared experience that one can enlarge his repertoire of the known, and thus make decisions which draw upon a wider base of fact and information. The importance of shared experience in decision-making grows more apparent every year, indeed, every day. For, in a hetero-

TABLE I
Two Contrasting Approaches to Teaching Composition

	The Traditional Approach	The Personal Growth Approach
MOTIVATION	To develop skills for future use. To gain promotion. To avoid censure. To acquire favor. To outdo others in competition for grades and status.	The young person's desire to clarify his own interests, needs, perceptions of self—right now.
CONTENT	Generally assigned by the teacher. Frequently used to check mastery of reading assignment. Seldom of vital interest to most students.	Based on real concerns of the student. Responses to: Who am I? How am I perceived by others? How am I unique, how similar?
AUDIENCE	Teacher or lay reader. People unlikely to be influenced by the message.	People who may be influenced by the message: self and peers mostly; teacher, parents, politicians, newspaper readers occasionally.
TASK	Finished, unified compositions; polished writing. Emphasis on mechanical correctness and style.	Some finished compositions in form of letters, articles, poems, etc. Many bits and pieces —lists, phrases, snatches of dialogue, etc.
REWARDS	Comments from reader (often negative, often directed toward pointing out errors) Publication (occasionally) Grades	The task itself. Feedback from audience. No rating of responses.

TABLE II
A Rank Ordering of Goals in Teaching Composition

1. To confirm to students that their perceptions are worthy of attention.
2. To help students process their perceptions into words, phrases, sentences, and longer sequences in order to clarify their thoughts and feelings, heighten their self-awareness and personal effectiveness.
3. To show that writing, a tool for extending the power of one's ears and voice, increases one's control over his environment and over his own growth and destiny.
4. To help students gain access to large bodies of assorted data, facts, images, statistics, quotations, etc.
5. To help students draw inferences from large bodies of data.
6. To help master specific skills for communicating their perceptions to others—skills of illustration, organization, emphasis, and comparison.
7. To help students develop precise, functional vocabularies.
8. To help students develop facility with complete sentence structures.
9. To help students master devices for gaining clarity, such as reference, parallelism, agreement, and punctuation.
10. To help students master such conventions as spelling, punctuation, and capitalization.

geneous world in which there is no generally agreed-upon system of values, and in which the choices confronting us are becoming increasingly numerous, complex, and pressing, our ability to make decisions about both our individual, personal futures and our collective, social future is more and more taxed.

These, then, are the goals of personal growth through

> **TABLE III**
>
> **Principles of the Personal Growth Approach to Composition**
>
> 1. The reason for teaching composition is to help the student to know himself and his world.
> 2. Knowledge of self and world can be divided into three skill areas: *Is this sequential?*
>   a. Composing our inner selves to find out who we are. (Identity)
>   b. Sharing experience, and growing by sharing with others. (Interpersonal relations)
>   c. Discovering what we value, and implementing our values in our daily lives. (Values into action)
> 3. The act of composition requires a subject perceived as meaningful by the composer.
> 4. The act of composition requires a responsive audience.
> 5. Growth through composition is best achieved through descriptive feedback and response to that feedback.
> 6. Peer feedback is a rich (and usually untapped) resource in the developing of composition skills.
> 7. Teachers can best stimulate growth through composition in the following ways:
>   a. By introducing engaging and stimulating activities and materials and relevant information.
>   b. By facilitating the group processes.
>   c. By clarifying problems which the students have encountered but cannot solve alone.
>   d. By offering additional feedback from a perspective which is experientially different from that of the student's peers.

composition: to compose our inner selves, to find out who we are; to grow by the sharing of experience with others; to discover what we value; and to learn how to make our lives reflect our values. *GOALS*

21

Name, Activities, relations (family), Achievements

2

Identity

ASK A YOUNG PERSON, "Who are you?" Chances are, he'll give you his name. Keep at it; ask him to give you ten answers. His answers will probably include items such as: a student, a football player, a part-time waiter, son of Mr. and Mrs. Jones, brother of Billy, someone who got a 74 on his math exam, a babysitter. And he probably won't reach ten.

We tend to think of ourselves in terms of our activities (a babysitter), our relationships (brother of Billy), and our achievements (a 74-getter); but we have almost no vocabulary that helps us identify ourselves in terms of what we feel, how we respond, what we value. We have very limited means of describing or knowing what kinds of people we really are.

The self-concepts that make up our identity keep shifting and rearranging themselves, much like the view in a kaleidoscope shifts and changes with each slight move.

Identity formation is a continuous and complex process which requires observation and reflection. The young person's judgment of himself is influenced by his perception of how others judge him. At the same time, he judges their judgment of him. Most of this boomeranging process is carried on unconsciously. Furthermore, the individual is constantly changing his self-concept as he becomes involved with an ever-widening circle of

IDENTITY [23

others who are significant to him. Thus, developing one's identity is a changing, growing process. Perhaps the most important attitudes that can be fostered are a tolerance for change and an acceptance of the possibilities for change in one's self.

AWARENESS AND SELF-CONFIDENCE

One of the most important ingredients for forging an identity is self-confidence. This should not be thought of as bolstering up weak egos for the sake of making young people feel better. Nor is it an attempt to make people function better by allowing them to conceal their tensions and anxieties. A weak ego does not gain much strength from being constantly pumped up. On the other hand, the strong, healthy ego resists artificiality and inflation. True self-confidence comes from an awareness of reality, an awareness of one's areas and degrees of competence and of one's areas and degrees of weakness. With this awareness one can plan for the future and provide for growth. The development of self-confidence through realistic self-awareness is one of the aims of *Composition for Personal Growth*.

In this chapter are described specific activities that a teacher can initiate to help students in their process of forming a personal identity.

One useful way for the teacher to look at identity is in terms of the Jo-Hari Model of Awareness in Interpersonal Relations.[1] The model is a grid divided into four cells which represent the self.

---

1. Luft, Joe, *Of Human Interaction*, Palo Alto: National Press Books, 1969.

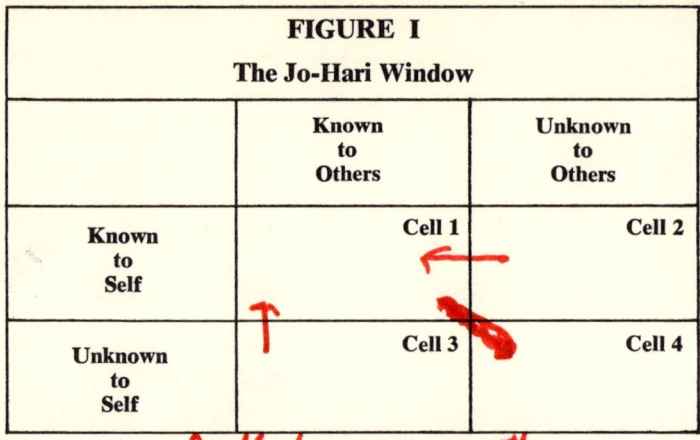

Growth in self-knowledge occurs when aspects in Cell Three advance into the area of Cell One; that is, when the individual learns some of the things which were known only to others. He can accomplish this through feedback from others—by listening and watching with more understanding, and by encouraging others to tell and show him things that they normally avoid or neglect to tell.

Generally this advance is stimulated by an accompanying move from Cell Two into Cell One, that is, by sharing with others some of the things that we formerly hid from them. This is the compensation for risk-taking. The individual who reveals some of the self known only to himself, in turn has revealed to him some of the self known only to others. And it is possible that through this collaborative sharing some light can be thrown into the corners of the dark and mysterious Cell Four, that area of self which is hidden from all.

Another useful way for the teacher to look at identity is in terms of The Three Rings of Self (Figure II).[2]

2. Attributed to Dr. Timothy Leary.

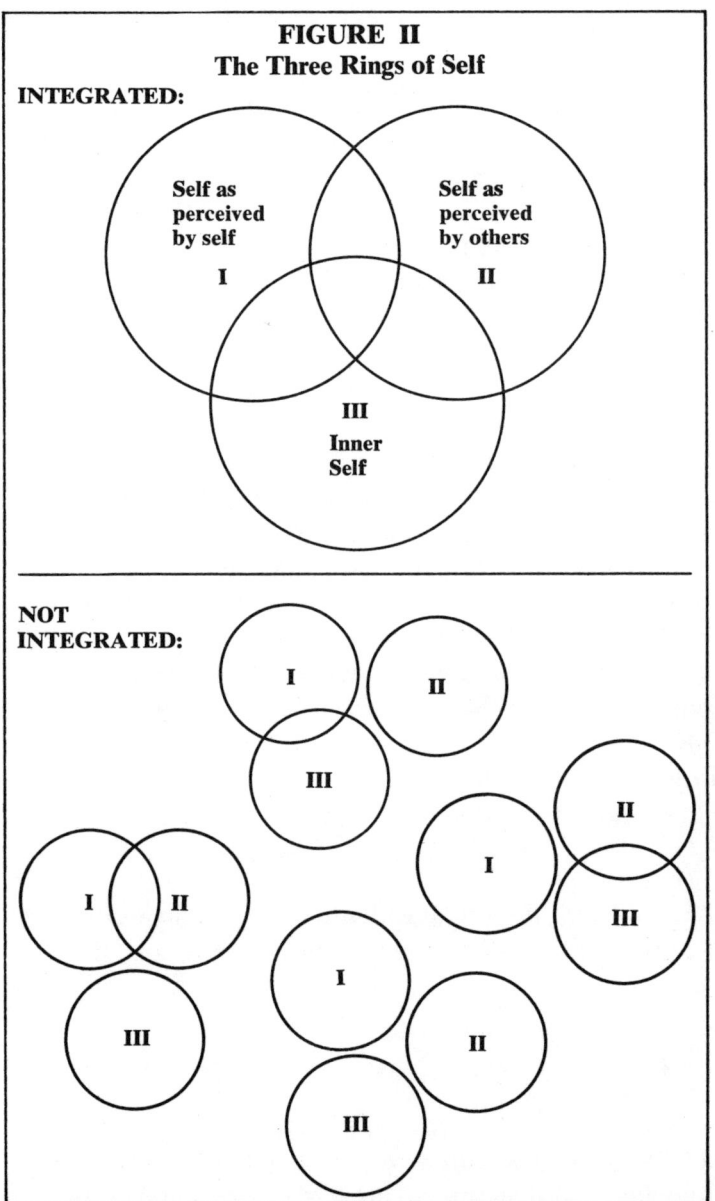

When the three rings of self are congruent, that is when the three rings describe the self in similar terms, then all is in harmony, and mental health is the result. When any one of the three rings describes a self which is not compatible with the other two, then the selves are pulling against each other and there is conflict within the person. And when all three rings describe different selves, the personality is totally disorganized.

Thus, a person whose behavior is perceived as bizarre by others is not necessarily mentally disturbed if it is his inner nature to be bizarre and if he realizes that his behavior is bizarre. On the other hand, if he is unaware that his behavior and inner self are bizarre, while others perceive them to be so, then he misperceives reality and may be mentally ill. If his inner self and his self-perception are congruent, but are at variance with how others perceive him, then there is a breakdown in communication between himself and others, with all the attendant consequences. And if he perceives himself as others do, but this perception is in conflict with his inner self, then the struggle between the inner and the social self will lead to some kind of breakdown.

AREAS OF IDENTITY

In order to investigate identity—or self-awareness—it is convenient to break it up into the following areas:

1. Patterns and preferences
2. Influences
3. Competencies
4. Body

Obviously these categories often overlap, but isolating them helps to structure an otherwise amorphous subject.

In the four sections which follow, some pertinent questions are raised related to each of these areas of identity. The questions are followed by suggestions for classroom activities which generate answers to these and other relevant questions. The activities have been listed in the area where they seem to have major emphasis, but each activity included is actually relevant to more than one area.

Important Note:

Many of the activities which follow call for the sharing of personal desires, feelings, hopes, etc. Students should understand (and be frequently reminded) that they are not required to respond if they prefer not to. The teacher should always explain the entire procedure for the activity at the beginning so that the students know in advance what risks are likely to be involved. When written responses are called for, the teacher must always specify whether it is to be public writing to be shared, or private writing for the author's eyes only. A student may, if he wishes, share his private writing, but he should never be forced to do so.

Area 1. PATTERNS AND PREFERENCES

Questions

What patterns can I observe in my behavior? To what extent are these patterns the result of conscious planning, and to what extent are they the result of just drifting? How can I regulate these patterns so that they are congruent with my feelings, preferences, values? What choices do I make? What do I prize and cherish? What are my desires? What unconscious desires do I repress?

What desires do I have that I feel I should resist? What characteristics do I possess which will help me live in closer accord with those values which I prize and cherish?

Activities

MAGIC BOX

The teacher instructs students as follows: In front of you is a box with indeterminate dimensions. This box is capable of delivering to you the one thing that will make you very happy. What is it?"

Students write their responses on unsigned 4 × 6 cards. They then arrange themselves in groups. One student in each group collects the cards and reads them aloud to the group, and all try to guess the author. This activity works best in groups of 5-8 people.

INVENTING A STORY[3]

Each student is asked to make up a story of no more than five to eight sentences about a boy and a violin (or any other comparable set of elements). The students form small groups. One person in each group collects and reads the stories aloud. The authors are not identified, but the group discusses what each story reveals about the author's attitudes, values, and past experiences.

FIVE THINGS THAT MAKE YOU FEEL GOOD

The students form small groups. Each student lists five specific things that members of his group can do that will make him feel good (e.g. "Reassure me—by nodding, winking, or signalling in some way—when you agree with

---

3. Malamud, D. I. & Machover, S. *Toward Self-Understanding: Group Techniques in Self-Confrontation*, Springfield Ill., Charles C. Thomas, 1965.

what I'm saying"). Each person reads his list aloud. The group makes a commitment: "Whenever we can honestly do so, we will try to do these things for one another."

CARD-SORT CENTER

Teacher (or aide, or student) creates stacks of cards, each card containing a word pair, such as the following:

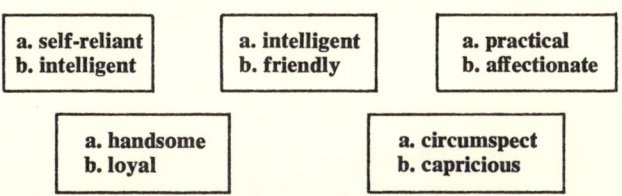

A question is placed on a table along with a stack of cards like those above. Sample questions:

1. Do you think of yourself as more *a* or more *b*?

2. Would you prefer to be more *a* or more *b*?

3. Do your acquaintances think of you as more *a* or more *b*?

Students move from table to table answering the questions by recording *a* or *b* on the reverse side of each card. They may tabulate the responses and see if norms emerge.

This is a good activity to have available in the classroom to be used at odd moments by individuals or small groups who have finished an assigned activity before the rest of the class.

Students should be encouraged to write "I Learned..." statements in their journals in relation to this activity. 4 × 6 cards should be available for anyone wishing to post his reactions or insights.

WHO AM I

The teacher asks the members of the class to close their eyes and see what first comes to mind in answer to the question: "Who am I?" After they have reflected on this question for thirty seconds or so, the teacher asks them to open their eyes and write a brief statement telling "Who I am." The statements can be shared in small groups.

ANGER

Each student is asked to write brief accounts of the last three times he was angry. These accounts are shared in small groups. Then each student estimates the number of times he becomes irritated or annoyed during an average week. A chart showing the frequency distribution of these estimates is placed on the blackboard and discussed.

DEVISING SENTENCES WITH HOMONYMS

The teacher reads out three words and instructs the students to make up a sentence using the three given words [e.g. steal (steel), watch, bear, (bare)]. After the group has written several such sentences for sets of given words, each student reads off his sentence for a given set. The group compares and discusses the individual differences noted. For example, were there different interpretations of the meanings and spellings of the words? How varied was the content? Students then read through their own sentences searching for patterns in expression or content.

Some other words with homonyms and multiple meanings that may be used for this exercise:

| route/root | hear/here | fine |
| red/read | saw | figure |

IDENTITY   [31

bat	so/sew	fast
chest	sign	point
grass	sight/site	pen

LISTING EMOTIONS

Each number of the class lists as many words that describe emotions as he can think of within one minute's time. The teacher asks the students to count the number of emotions they listed. Students next count up the number of positive emotions on their lists and the number that are negative. They discuss what a preponderance in one direction or the other might reflect.

ADDITIONAL ACTIVITIES

The activities which follow are largely individual projects. Some call for sharing and group discussion as a final activity, but, for the most part, they are to be done by each student alone. At the conclusion of each activity, students should save their worksheet(s) in their journals for later reference and for comparing their future responses with their past responses to the same or similar activities. The general procedure the teacher follows for these activities is to explain the activity briefly, hand out the worksheets, and remain available to answer questions that may arise.

DEFINING SUCCESS

Instruction Sheet

1. Examine the worksheet to see how important each of the items is to you. Copy the items into your journal in the order of their importance to you.

2. Choose the four items on the list that you consider the most important and place a 1 beside these items

on the worksheet; place a 2 beside four items next in importance to you; a 3 next to the four next important items; a 4 next to the next four important items; and a 5 next to the four least important items.

3. Make a quick guess at how these items would be ranked by other students of your sex. Mark each item with numbers 1 through 5 in the appropriate column.

4. Make a quick guess at how these items would be ranked by others of the opposite sex. Record your guesses in the appropriate column on the worksheet.

5. Indicate your sex at the top of the worksheet and make up your code number. Your code should be a six digit number of your own choosing—be sure to make a note of it so that you will be able to retrieve your worksheet later.

6. Give the worksheet to the teacher.

7. In your journal, place an *N* beside each item on the list which is present in your life right now.

8. Place a *D* beside any item you doubt you will be able to attain.

9. Are there any items of importance to you that are absent from this list? Add these items to the list in your journal.

10. Examine your ratings for patterns. *make more specific*

11. Compose "I Learned . . ." statements. (See p. 35)

12. Share some "I Learned . . ." statements with your group.

DEFINING SUCCESS
Worksheet

your sex (M or F)   your code

Success means:	Anticipated ratings by others of your sex	Anticipated ratings by others of opposite sex	Your ratings
1. Having worthy offspring			
2. Enjoying an active and satisfying sex life			
3. Being able to influence others			
4. Being able to draw love from others			
5. Having power over things (e.g. being able to fix a car, build a boat, program a computer)			
6. Having artistic skill			
7. Engaging in active and satisfying athletic activity			
8. Having opportunities for risk and adventure			
9. Displaying intellectual competence			
10. Enjoying good health			

(continued on following page)

DEFINING SUCCESS
Worksheet

your sex (M or F)   your code

Success means:	Anticipated ratings by others of your sex	Anticipated ratings by others of opposite sex	Your ratings
11. Possession of pleasure-yielding inanimate objects e.g. new leather belt, hand-carved chess set, Triumph 650)			
12. Winning approval of opposite sex			
13. Being stimulated intellectually			
14. Being physically attractive			
15. Achieving prestige			
16. Being able to initiate and sustain friendships			
17. Resilience (being able to bounce back)			
18. Being able to give love			
19. Being involved in socially significant activity			
20. Enjoying a close and supportive family life			

When students have completed this activity, the teacher and/or the students can do some statistical analysis of the worksheets to determine patterns of response for the class. The results will provide fuel for much follow-up discussion.

SATISFYING LEARNING EXPERIENCES

Instruction Sheet

1. Think of the eight most satisfying learning experiences that you have ever had. (These may or may not be part of your school experience; for example learning to ride a bike, or tie your shoe.)
2. In the spaces numbered one through eight, write a word to identify each of the eight experiences.
3. Examine each experience and check each statement that would apply.
4. Total the checks across.
5. Now review your list and the totalled checks. Write a few sentences describing your most satisfying learning styles.

SATISFYING LEARNING Worksheet									
	1	2	3	4	5	6	7	8	TOTAL
I acquired INFORMATION									
I acquired CONCEPT(S)									
I acquired SKILL(S)									
I was PHYSICALLY IN MOTION									
I gained power over THINGS									
I gained power over PEOPLE									
I gained power over SELF									
I knew in ADVANCE what I wanted to learn									
PERSEVERANCE was involved									
An OUTSIDE EVALUATION was not important									
I proved myself to MYSELF									
I impressed OTHERS									
I received a TANGIBLE REWARD									

FRIENDS

1. List characteristics that you consider essential in the ideal friend:

2. Number these characteristics in the order of their importance to you.
3. Enter the names of peers you associate with most frequently on the lettered lines below. Enter your ranked characteristics of the ideal friend at the top of the numbered columns. Examine each name in light of the characteristics you have listed. Place checks in appropriate squares.

Name	1	2	3	4	5	6	7	8	9	10
A.										
B.										
C.										
D.										
E.										
F.										
G.										
H.										
I.										
J.										

4. Examine the checks on the preceding page. What patterns do you detect?
5. Compose "I Learned..." statements for your journal.

PREFERENCES

1. List twenty or so things you really love doing:

	$	A	N	M	Date
1.					
2.					
3.					
4.					
5.					
6.					
7.					
8.					
9.					
10.					
11.					
12.					
13.					
14.					
15.					
16.					
17.					
18.					
19.					
20.					

IDENTITY   [39

2. Think about the things you listed for the next several days. Add and subtract items until you are satisfied with your list.
3. Put a star beside the five most loved entries.
4. Add to the list five things you have not done but are fairly sure you would love doing.
5. The symbols at the top of the columns stand for:
   $ = costs more than $5 to do
   A = you prefer to do this alone
   N = this activity would not be on your list four years from now
   M = your mother would approve of you for loving this

   Go down your list of activities and check all the appropriate boxes.

6. In the fifth column headed "Date," write 1, 2, or 3:
   1 for any item you have done within the past week.
   2 for any item you have done within the past month.
   3 if it has been more than a month since you've done this.
7. Think of a person who has been a great influence in your life. Which items would this person disapprove of you for loving? Write D beside these items.
8. Write +5 beside any item you expect will be missing from your list five years from now, and −5 beside any item that would not have been on your list five years ago.
9. Put W beside any item that you love to do but really wish you didn't (e.g. smoking).
10. Look at the five things you would like to do but

have not done. Describe briefly below what keeps you from doing each of these activities.

11. Write "I Learned . . ." statement(s) in your journal.

This activity can be repeated after a month and the two lists compared. What things are missing from or have been added to the second list? Is there a significant change in the order in which items are listed?

EXCITING MOMENTS

1. List the ten most <u>thrilling or exciting</u> moments you have experienced during the last six years.
2. List several exciting moments from earlier years.
3. Do you detect any patterns? <u>What conditions need to be present in order for you to experience high excitement?</u>

HAPPY MOMENTS

1. Divide your age into three approximately equal spans of time. List the five happiest moments for each span.

Early Years
(Birth to age ___)

1. _____
2. _____
3. _____
4. _____
5. _____

Middle Years
(Age ___ to age ___)

1. _____
2. _____
3. _____
4. _____
5. _____

Recent Years
(Age ___ to present)

1. _____
2. _____
3. _____
4. _____
5. _____

2. Use the characteristics below, or make up your own set, and put the appropriate symbols next to the items on your list.
   A = alone
   O = with others
   W = won approval
   R = won tangible reward
   E = experienced something for the first time

Area 2: INFLUENCES

Questions

What influences have caused me to perceive myself as

42] COMPOSITION FOR PERSONAL GROWTH

I do? How has my mother influenced my self-concept? How have my father, siblings, peers, teachers, priest, newspapers, television, magazines, advertisements, local climate, native language influenced what I am? How have these influences affected my values and beliefs?

Activities

MAGAZINE STEREOTYPES

Teacher instructs students to bring to class three issues of a magazine they read or that their parents subscribe to. Examining only advertisements and pictures, students list characteristics of the stereotyped male teenager, female teenager, father, mother, grandparent as portrayed in the magazine.

TALKING WITH PARENTS

The teacher asks the students to close their eyes and to remember from their childhood a conversation with Mother. The students write out the verbal exchange on unsigned index cards. They form small groups. The cards are collected and read aloud and discussed.

FAMILY SAYINGS

The teacher starts the discussion by stating that every family has its own favorite expressions, proverbs, slogans, words of advice, admonitions, superstitions. He may give a personal example, such as: "What will people think?" He then asks the group to close their eyes and see what repetitive sayings pop into mind. Each student writes out his family's slogans, along with any identifying data he remembers, such as who said it most often. Small groups are formed and students read off their lists of family sayings and compare notes.

"I AM... THE GROUP SEES ME AS..." STATEMENTS

Each student writes on one side of a 4 × 6 card five sentences describing some of his personal characteristics, e.g.

> I am loyal to a fault, always excusing my friends' mistakes.
>
> I am always prompt for appointments.
>
> I am hypercritical. I am never satisfied with what I do and always think that others do better.
>
> I am easy to get along with.
>
> I am eager to please.

On the other side of the card he writes five sentences describing how he imagines the group sees him, e.g.

> The group sees me as weak.
>
> The group sees me as even-tempered.
>
> The group sees me as the last one you ask to join your team.
>
> The group sees me as compulsive.
>
> The group sees me as good-natured.

The card is left unsigned. Small groups are formed. Everyone hands in his card and the cards are distributed randomly to the members of the group. All the "I am..." sides are read aloud one after the other. The group guesses who wrote which. Then, more slowly, each card is read again. The writer declares himself, and the other side is read. The group corroborates or takes issue with the statements attributed to it.

After this discussion, each student records his reactions in his journal.

INFLUENCES

1. List the names of ten peers for whom you have great respect:

    1. _____
    2. _____
    3. _____
    4. _____
    5. _____
    6. _____
    7. _____
    8. _____
    9. _____
    10. _____

Examine your list. What qualities do you regard as important in a peer?

2. List the names of ten adults you know for whom you have great respect.

    1. _____
    2. _____
    3. _____
    4. _____

5. _____
6. _____
7. _____
8. _____
9. _____
10. _____

What qualities do you value in an adult?

3. Compare the two lists of qualities, and compose an "I Learned..." statement.

4. List up to ten people who have warm affection for you:

1. _____
2. _____
3. _____
4. _____
5. _____
6. _____
7. _____
8. _____
9. _____
10. _____

5. Of all the peers and adults you have listed, which five have had the greatest influence on your values:

1. _____
2. _____
3. _____
4. _____
5. _____

Are there more peers than adults on this list, or vice versa? Do most of the names on this list come from list number 1, 2 or 4? Compose an "I Learned . . ." statement.

COMMANDMENTS

The Ten Commandments are listed in the Bible. The Boy Scout and Girl Scout handbooks list commandments. In everyday life, commandments are more frequently left unstated, although their force is clearly felt.

1. List the ten commandments of your family:

1. _____
2. _____
3. _____
4. _____
5. _____
6. _____
7. _____
8. _____
9. _____
10. _____

2. List the ten commandments of your school:

   1. _____
   2. _____
   3. _____
   4. _____
   5. _____
   6. _____
   7. _____
   8. _____
   9. _____
   10. _____

3. List the ten commandments of your peers:

   1. _____
   2. _____
   3. _____
   4. _____
   5. _____
   6. _____
   7. _____
   8. _____
   9. _____
   10. _____

4. List the ten commandments by which your teachers live:

   1. _____
   2. _____
   3. _____
   4. _____
   5. _____
   6. _____
   7. _____
   8. _____
   9. _____
   10. _____

5. List ten commandments you would like to live by:

   1. _____
   2. _____
   3. _____
   4. _____
   5. _____
   6. _____
   7. _____
   8. _____
   9. _____
   10. _____

6. Star one or two commandments you would particularly like to work on. Consider writing a Self-Contract.

Area 3: COMPETENCIES[4]

Questions

What is my ability to perceive experiences with objectivity, sensitivity and depth? What is my ability to organize and store perceived experience for my present and future needs? What is my psycho-motor competence, in terms of body movement and control? What is my cognitive competence, my ability to understand, organize and generalize the complexities of this universe? What is my affective competence, my ability to know and to organize what I feel? What is my social competence, my ability to perceive and understand patterns of relationships among people? What is my volitional competence, my ability to define my goals and aspirations, and my perseverance in attaining those aspirations? And what is my esthetic competence, my ability to grasp the underlying order of things and to build and reorder things creatively?

Activities

SECRETS

Each person writes a secret hope, fear, wish on an unsigned piece of paper, folds the paper four times, and drops it into a box. The box is shuffled. Each person in turn draws a secret from the box, unfolds the paper, and

---

4. For a more detailed discussion of competencies see Daniel C. Jordan, "The ANISA Model—A New Educational System for Releasing Human Potential," *The American Oxonian*, LVII (1070), 542-554.

reads the secret aloud. He then talks about the secret as if the hopes, fears, aspirations, feelings expressed were his own. If someone happens to draw his own secret, he may either pass or read it as if it were someone else's.

Following this activity, each person should record his responses in his journal.

ARM DROP

Teacher asks the class, "If someone were to try to lift your arm and drop it, how much control would you exercise? Can you consciously control your emotions and your muscles? Is this easy? Do right and left arms differ?"

Students pair up. One partner assumes a relaxed stance and the other gently lifts and drops one of his arms. The person whose arm is being lifted focuses on his own ability to give up muscular control; the dropper focuses on how his handling creates or eases tension.

After roles are reversed several times, students record their reactions in their journals. Discussion is encouraged in small groups about the extent to which emotional behavior can be affected by will. Students can record in their journals observations about what their behavior in this exercise reveals about how they act in real life.

HAVE YOU NOTICED?

Each student pairs off with someone he does not know well. Each pair joins another pair they do not know well. Everyone fills out the following questionnaire testing powers of observation. The foursome then discuss their answers.

OBSERVATION QUESTIONNAIRE

1. Does your house door swing outward or inward?
2. At what time of day is the traffic heaviest on your street?
3. Does your father (mother, or brother or sister) eat one food at a time at dinner, or does he eat them all together? (That is, would he eat all his meat before trying his potatoes, or would he eat a bit of meat and then a bit of potatoes, etc.?)
4. Which arm do you put through your coat sleeve first? How about legs into trousers?
5. When you fold your arms across your chest, is your right arm over your left arm, or vice-versa? Do all right-handed (left-handed) people do it that way?
6. If a book has an introduction and a preface, which comes first?
7. Do birds stop singing before or after sunset in the summer?
8. Which shoe do you put on first when you dress in the morning? Do you always do it that way?
9. Who among your classmates is usually the last one to arrive at school in the morning?
10. Who among your classmates is the slowest eater?
11. Which color is your mother least likely to wear?
12. Who among your classmates wears the greatest variety of clothing in an average week?
13. Is the taste of food more distinct when it is hot or when it is cold?

Each foursome makes up several more observation test items, which may be collected for future use.

Students record "I Learned . . ." statements in their journals.

WHAT AM I GOOD AT?

Each student is asked to list thirty things that he is good at. Then he looks over his list and devises a classification scheme to organize his list of competencies. (e.g. Physical, Social, Intellectual; or, Outdoors, Indoors, At School, At Home, At Work, Alone, With Others; Self-Initiated, Assigned, etc.)

The group then shares their organization schemes and discusses individual and group tendencies that emerge.

ACCOMPLISHMENTS

1. Divide your age into three equal spans. For each time span, list five accomplishments that you are proud of and that you really wanted to do.
2. In the first column, rank the accomplishments in order of their importance to you.
3. In the second column, enter P if the accomplishment involved working with people, or TH if it involved things.
4. In the third column, use the following symbols to describe each accomplishment:
   D = overcame *d*ifficulties
   H = *h*elped people
   C = *c*reated, innovated
   A = demonstrated *a*bility
5. In the fourth column, use the following symbols to

	Rank	P or TH	D/H/C/A	T/I/L/M	*
Early Years (Birth to age ___)					
1.					
2.					
3.					
4.					
5.					
Middle Years (Age ___ to age ___)					
1.					
2.					
3.					
4.					
5.					
Recent Years (Age ___ to present)					
1.					
2.					
3.					
4.					
5.					

characterize each accomplishment:
T = worked as a *t*eam member
I = worked *i*ndividually
L = was a *l*eader
M = was a *m*anager (organizer of people or things)

6. In the last column, place a star beside each accomplishment that involved triumphing over others in competition.

7. Reread your list of accomplishments and answer the following questions:
   a. What factors influenced your choice of activities?
   b. What factors helped you persevere?
   c. What rewards did you receive for your accomplishments? What punishments would have resulted had you not succeeded?
   d. Compose "I Learned . . ." statements based on your answers to these questions.

8. List the names of any people who helped you significantly. Consider writing to them.

9. List five activities you might want to undertake in the future that you think would bring you success and satisfaction.

Area 4: BODY

Questions

To what extent am I aware of my body—of its strengths and weaknesses? To what extent do I accept its limitations?

Activities

OFFSPRING, AGED SIXTEEN

The teacher asks the students to close their eyes and imagine what they would like an offspring of theirs to look like at age sixteen. Then, being as specific as possible, students write a paragraph describing that offspring.

The paragraphs are read anonymously in the small groups, and the group tries to guess each author.

Then, using a Revealed Differences Survey (see page 00) the teacher can ask how many boys pictured their offspring as male, how many as female. The same question is asked of the girls. Other revealed difference questions: How many blonds saw their offspring as blonds; curly-haired as curly-haired; brown-eyed as brown-eyed; etc.

LEMONS

The teacher passes out lemons to each member of the group. Students are told to get familiar with their lemons by feeling the shape and texture with closed eyes. After five minutes, the lemons are placed in a basket and each student is asked to find his lemon from the collection, eyes closed. The lemons should be marked so that positive identification can be made. (Almost everybody finds his own lemon!) After this activity the teacher might ask each student to write a description telling what helped him differentiate his lemon from the other lemons.

ARM AND HAND

Students are asked to list in their journals five things that they are proud that their arms and hands can do.

They then pair off and examine each other's hands

and arms from the elbow down, noting all the individual characteristics. Right and left arms and hands are compared for size and other differences.

Each student then writes a brief paragraph describing his own or his partner's hand. Groups of three or four pairs are formed, and one person reads all the descriptions. Members guess whose hand is being described.

BODY CHANGES

Students are asked to list eight changes that they would like to make in their bodies to improve them. Then they are asked to list five changes that they would not like to see happen (ruling out disfiguration from accident or disease).

They form small groups and share whatever items they feel they can.

The teacher may use the Revealed Differences technique to find out, for example, how many would like to be taller, how many thinner, how many would change the color of their eyes, etc.

BLINDFOLDED CONVERSATION

Small groups are formed and each person puts on a blindfold or closes his eyes. They carry on a conversation about an assigned topic. They are to try to be as aware as possible of how the loss of sight affects their ability to converse.

The topic for conversation must be a compelling one. Here is a suggested topic: The group is about to be cast away on an island which has ample resources to take care of bodily needs (food, shelter). The group has ten minutes to decide which six of these ten items should be taken with them to the island: a football; the complete works of Shakespeare; a pack of playing cards; a chess set; a mirror; a set of oil paints; a harmonica; a typewriter with a supply of paper; a water bed; a badminton set. Students are asked to think about the list for one minute without talking, then to carry on their discussion with closed eyes and reach consensus in ten minutes.

IDENTITY: GENERAL

Here are some additional activities which offer experiences in self-awareness. They may be used in conjunction with other identity activities or independently. These activities are time-consuming and should be undertaken when enough time can be allowed for students to formulate their ideas.

YOUR PERSONAL COAT OF ARMS[5]

In each area on your coat of arms, make a drawing to express your thought. Do not use words except for 6. Your drawings can be simple, incomplete, and even unintelligible to others, as long as they express your feelings.

---

5. Adapted from a suggestion by Sister Louise, St. Juliana's School, Chicago.

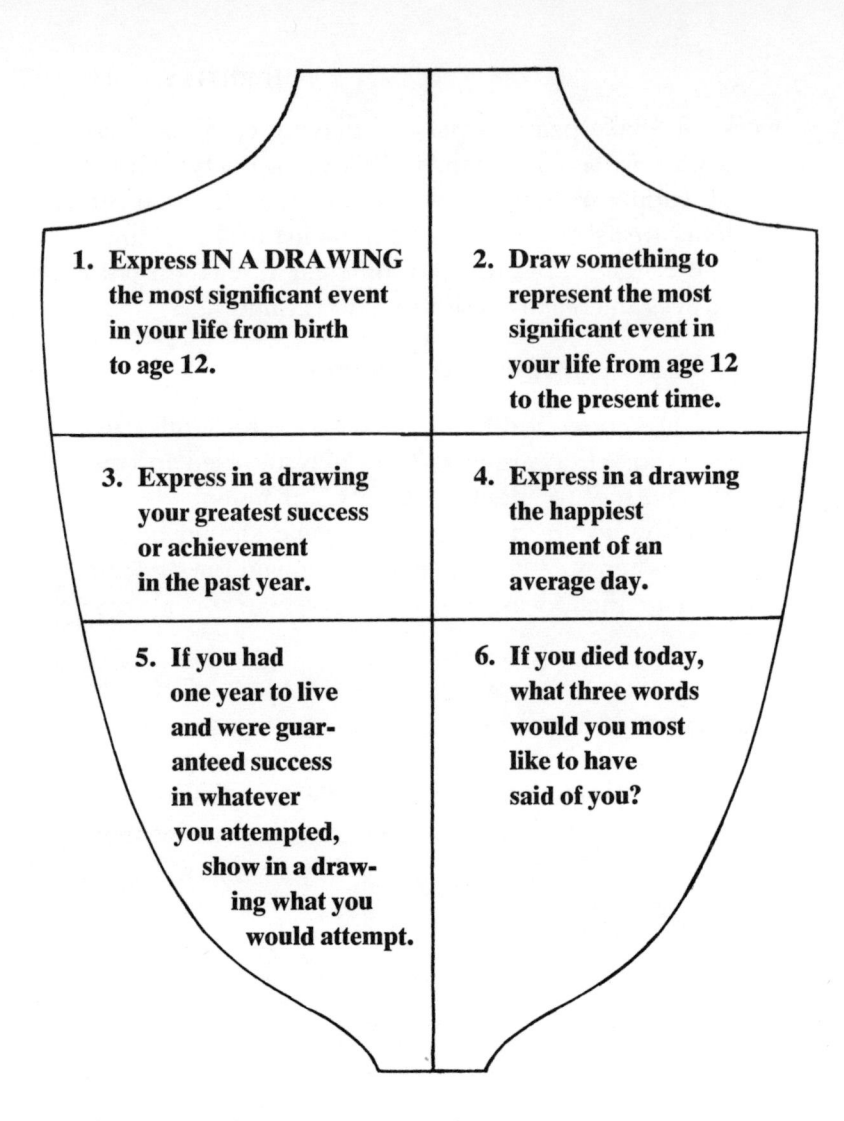

1. **Express IN A DRAWING the most significant event in your life from birth to age 12.**

2. **Draw something to represent the most significant event in your life from age 12 to the present time.**

3. **Express in a drawing your greatest success or achievement in the past year.**

4. **Express in a drawing the happiest moment of an average day.**

5. **If you had one year to live and were guaranteed success in whatever you attempted, show in a drawing what you would attempt.**

6. **If you died today, what three words would you most like to have said of you?**

Share your drawings with the members of the group. Make up "I Learned..." statements.

SATISFYING EXPERIENCES I
1. List the twelve most satisfying experiences that you have had in the last few years.
2. Using the code below, place a check in every box that is appropriate for each experience.
3. Examine your worksheet. What patterns can you find in your most satisfying experiences?
4. Compose one or more "I Learned..." statements for your journal.

Experience	MY EFFORT						MY REWARD						
	A	B	C	D	E	F	G	H	I	J	K	L	M
1.													
2.													
3.													
4.													
5.													
6.													
7.													
8.													
9.													
10.													
11.													
12.													

MY EFFORT:

A. I used physical skill
B. I used intellectual skills
C. I used social skills
D. I knew what I wanted
E. I tried hard to succeed
F. I took a risk

MY REWARDS:

G. I proved myself to myself
H. I impressed others
I. I received warmth and affection
J. I received sensual pleasure
K. I achieved recognition
L. I received a tangible reward
M. I did well in competition with others

SATISFYING EXPERIENCES II

1. Read the list of qualities and rank order them from 1 to 20 in order of their importance to you as they describe your *best* self.

2. Identify the six most satisfying experiences that you have had in the last two years.

3. For each experience, check the six qualities which best describe you in that experience. (You may check fewer than six, but never more than six for any one experience.)

4. Compose one or more "I Learned . . ." statements, for your journal.

Qualities	Rank	Experience #1	Experience #2	Experience #3	Experience #4	Experience #5	Experience #6
ADVENTURESOME (experimental, daring)							
AMBITIOUS (striving, aspiring)							
BROADMINDED (open-minded)							
CAPABLE (competent, effective)							
CHEERFUL (lighthearted, joyful)							
COMPETITIVE (driving)							
CONSIDERATE (courteous, well-mannered)							
COURAGEOUS (standing up in face of fear)							
CREATIVE (imaginative)							
FORGIVING (not holding grudges)							
HELPFUL (altruistic, working for others)							
HONEST (sincere, truthful)							
INDEPENDENT (self-reliant, self-sufficient)							
INTELLECTUAL (intelligent, reflective)							
LOGICAL (consistent, rational)							
LOVING (affectionate, tender)							
OBEDIENT (dutiful, respectful)							
RESPONSIBLE (dependable, reliable)							
SELF-CONTROLLED (restrained, self-disciplined)							
SEXUALLY APPEALING (physically attractive)							

3

Interpersonal Relations

NO MAN IS AN ISLAND, and few can live without almost constant interaction with others. For an individual to grow and mature, he must be aware of the people around him and of their influence on his behavior and attitudes.

FUNDAMENTAL DYNAMICS

William C. Schutz identifies three key types of behavior involved in interpersonal relationships: inclusion, control, and affection.[1]

Inclusion behavior is directed toward satisfying the need for association with people—for companionship, for belonging, for togetherness. A person who is not included is often described as "isolated," "ignored," or "abandoned."

Control behavior is directed toward satisfying the need to exert authority or influence over other people. One who lacks control is described as a "follower," a "submissive person," or a "milquetoast"; while one who reacts negatively to controls is said to be "rebellious" or "unruly."

Affection behavior is directed toward satisfying the need for close, personal feelings between two people. Al-

---

[1] For a full treatment of this analysis see William C. Schutz, *A Three-Dimensional Theory of Interpersonal Behavior*, New York: Holt, Rinehart and Winston, 1960.

though inclusion and control behavior can occur between two people or between one person and a group, affection behavior can occur only between two people at a time. Some terms that connote a positive affective relationship are "love," "like," or "friendship;" while "hate" and "dislike" connote a negative affective relationship.

Difficulties in interpersonal relationships occur when any one of these variables becomes dominant. Thus, the "joiner," in attempting to be included in everything, is committed to nothing, whereas the "loner" isolates himself to his own detriment. The "dominator" attempts to force his will on the group, while the "milquetoast" is unwilling or unable to influence decisions. Such affectional types as the "blanket" and the "cadaver" need no comment.

ACCEPTANCE AND REJECTION

Another useful way of looking at interpersonal relationships is in terms of the decisions a person makes as a result of his need for acceptance and fear of rejection.[2] The person with a healthy view of life will be aware of his needs and fears and will recognize the need to risk rejection in order to fulfill the need for acceptance. And he will recognize that risk-taking inevitably involves losses as well as gains.

The maladapted person, on the other hand, is so afraid of rejection that he will not openly express his need for affection. Rather, he will alienate others so that they do not become tempted to offer him affection and accept-

---

2. For a treatment of this view in a somewhat different context see Karen Horney, *Neurosis and Human Growth*, New York: W. W. Norton, 1950.

ance and then disappoint him by withdrawing and rejecting him.

This alienation of others takes three forms: moving *toward* people by surrendering independence; moving *away* from people by withdrawing or resigning; and moving *against* people by attacking or aggravating. These three forms are well represented in young people today: moving toward by the overconforming, listless, inconsistent student; moving away by the apathetic, passive, drifting student; and moving against by the rebellious, hostile, overdissenting student.

AREAS OF INTERPERSONAL RELATIONS

Some of the questions that the personal-growth approach to composition attempts to deal with in terms of interpersonal relations are: How am I perceived by others? In what ways am I like, and in what ways unlike, others? How much influence do I have over others, and how can I be more influential? Am I satisfied with the quantity and quality of my friendships, and how can I improve my friendships? To what extent do I collaborate constructively with others, and how can I improve my collaborative efforts? How good am I at giving and receiving feedback, and how can I improve these skills? What is the value of self-disclosure, and when and how much should I reveal, how much conceal? What is the value of risk-taking, and when and where should I take risks? How good am I at listening, understanding, and empathizing, and how can I improve these skills?

INTERPERSONAL RELATIONS ACTIVITIES

"CLAY" SCULPTURE

In this nonverbal activity, one person becomes a piece

of "clay." Another person is the sculptor who molds the "clay" so that it reflects how he perceives the "clay's" personality. Observers jot down their perceptions of this interaction. In addition, they write a brief interpretation of the finished sculpture.

WHO WROTE WHICH STORIES?

The teacher asks each member of the class to write three stories (no longer than five sentences each)—one about a boy and a gun, a second about a teenage girl and a teacher, and a third about a young man and his employer.

He invites two students to volunteer to have their stories read to the group. After reading the two sets of stories, without identifying their authors, the teacher announces to the class, "I would like you to guess which set of stories was written by each of these two volunteers. Before making your decision, it will help you to interview each volunteer in turn about his childhood."

The interviewing and author-identification should be followed by a general discussion focusing on the criteria used in the questioning and decision-making processes. The activity can then be repeated with new volunteers.

STRENGTH BOMBARDMENT

The class is divided into small groups. Each student jots down all the good things he can think of about each of the other members of the group. Then, focusing on one individual at a time, the group tells each person the good things they have identified about him. There is no need to try to avoid repetition, and group members should feel free to add to their lists at any time. The one hard-and-fast rule for this activity is that *you must believe what you say.*

VARIATION OF STRENGTH BOMBARDMENT

After small groups have worked together on an activity, each person lists one or two specific behaviors of each other person in his group to which he responded positively. The procedure for STRENGTH BOMBARDMENT is then followed.

GUESSING EACH OTHER'S BEHAVIOR

Each student chooses several actual situations from his own life and outlines the experiences briefly. These are read to the group one at a time. The other members of the group try to guess how the writer reacted, what he felt and did in the situation reported. After the group has given its conjectures, the individual reveals how he really did react.

PAPER TOWER

The class is divided into groups of eight. Each group gets one stack of newspapers and one roll of masking tape. For fifteen minutes, each group plans a construction that will be judged for height, stability, and beauty (no physical work is permitted during the planning period). Twenty minutes are then allowed for construction.

The class examines all the constructions and judges them. After the judging is completed, students record in their journals answers to some of the following questions:

1. What percentage of the plan did you contribute?

2. What percentage could you have contributed?

3. Did your group have a leader? Who? How was he chosen? Characterize his style.

4. Which of the following words best describes your role in the planning session: wallflower, dominator,

facilitator, inventor, negativist, questioner, clarifier, humorist? Is there another word that describes you even better?

5. How were your ideas received during the planning session?
6. How did the group generally respond to all the ideas that were expressed?
7. List three specific behaviors exhibited during the planning session that you feel were helpful.
8. List one behavior *you* exhibited during the planning session that you feel was helpful.

Caution: Positive Focus

A word of caution to teachers: we all *know* our weaknesses. They cling to us like parasites, haunt us like ghosts. We lavish attention on them, nourish them, believe in them. And everywhere our civilization encourages us in this energy-wasting process. We need to be liberated from our weaknesses, not reminded of them. We need to feel more at ease in giving and receiving compliments, less anxious and suspicious.

A really nice compliment from a casual acquaintance comes, we think, from his desire to "butter me up," "to sell me something." When it comes from a close friend, the compliment is discredited as being offered "just to make me feel better," "to bolster my ego." Compliments that are obviously sincere and inescapably apt provoke all sorts of blushing, staring-at-the-floor, "shucks-it-was-nothing" behaviors. Giving and receiving positive feedback is so fraught with difficulties that many of us are unable to honestly engage in the process, and thus we reinforce each other's self-doubts.

As teachers we know that students flourish in an atmosphere of approval, wither and die in an atmosphere of disapproval. Nevertheless, we constantly find ourselves yielding to the pressures around us, focusing on the weaknesses of our students and colleagues.

The teacher using the personal growth program must be steadfast in resisting pressures to focus evenly on the positive *and* the negative. Day-to-day reality will more than even the balance. Furthermore, an "even" focus on both the positive and the negative actually has the effect of focusing on the negative. Given a paragraph of positive feedback and a paragraph of negative feedback, many persons will truly believe only the negative.

The vast number of writing activities in *Composition for Personal Growth* encourage a positive view of oneself and others. To be sure, in terms of cognition, an analysis of one's most shameful failures will offer insights just as significant as those offered by an analysis of one's most valued successes. But, while the former will be enervating and degrading, the latter will be exhilarating and liberating.

4

Values into Action

ONE OF THE MOST SIGNIFICANT and disturbing findings in values research is the fact that values, beliefs, and attitudes have little effect on behavior. Thus, a teacher may espouse student rights and personal freedom, yet be highly autocratic or manipulative in the conduct of his classes. Or students may believe in racial equality, yet do nothing to promote this value. Vast numbers of young people, confronted with a confusing array of choices and no clear-cut guidelines, drop out or drift along, refusing to make value decisions and allowing others to determine the course of their lives. And the choices which confront young people are rapidly becoming more numerous and more complex.

The ultimate concern of *Composition for Personal Growth* is with value exploration and clarification. Through composition, students can become more aware of congruence or disparity between their values and their actions; more aware of the forces causing disparity, and the skills needed to effect congruence.

THE SEVEN POINTS OF VALUING

The personal-growth approach to valuing delineates seven points—four related to choosing, and three related to acting.[1]

---

1. Adapted from Louis E. Raths, Merrill Harmin, and Sidney B. Simon, *Values and Teaching: Working with Values in the Classroom,* Columbus, Ohio: Charles E. Merrill Publishing Co., 1966, pp. 28-30.

In choosing a value, one should consider the four following points:

1. *Preferences:* What do I prefer? What do I prize and cherish?

2. *Alternatives:* What are the alternatives to this choice? Have I considered other options carefully?

3. *Influences:* How has my choice been influenced by others? To what degree is it an independent choice?

4. *Consequences:* What are the consequences of this choice? Am I willing to accept these consequences?

In translating the value into action, one should consider the following three points:

5. *Public Affirmation:* Am I willing to affirm this value publicly? Have I done so?

6. *Acting:* Am I willing to act upon this value? In what ways? Have I done so?

7. *Acting repeatedly:* Am I willing to act on this value so that it becomes a pattern in my life? In what ways have I established this value as a pattern for my life?

OPEN, ACCEPT, STIMULATE

The first step in helping a young person with his valuing process is to open up the whole subject of values; to stimulate him to examine his beliefs in value-related areas; and to encourage him to share his thoughts with others.

The next step is to accept the young person's thoughts, feelings, and beliefs nonjudgmentally, and to encourage students in the class to accept each other's views for what they are, without trying to change or criticize them. This helps the student to know that he can be honest with the teacher and the class, no matter how gloomy or confused his feelings might be.

And the third step is to stimulate additional thinking, so that the individual can move toward greater congruence between his values and his actions. Here the seven points of valuing and the questions they raise can aid in exploring and clarifying values.

AREAS OF CONCERN

Here are some common areas of concern to young persons. Questions and activities related to these areas can be expecially useful in stimulating value exploration and clarification.

Family: How can I break away from my parents without hurting them?

Love: Am I in love? What is love?

Sex: What? When? How far?

Money: How much should I try to save? How can I keep myself from wasting it?

Work: Should I try to get a summer job? What do I want to do as my life's work?

Leisure: How can I get more joy out of my leisure time?

Time: In what ways do I waste time? Is it really wasted?

Friendship: How close should I be with my friends? What should I do about former friends?

Goals: What are my personal goals? Are they realistic? Too high? Too low?

Drugs and Alcohol: Yes or no? What? When? Why?

Relationship to Authority: How can I live in harmony with authority without being false to myself? To what extent must I accept authority?

VALUES-INTO-ACTION ACTIVITIES

BRAINSTORMING VALUES INTO ACTION

The class is divided into groups. Members of groups are asked to write out ten values that they think they have in common. They can then select one value, and "brainstorm" ways to act upon that value. They then choose the best or most feasible items from the brainstorm list and talk about how they can implement these actions.

PUBLIC-AFFIRMATION LETTER WRITING

Using the values arrived at in the preceding exercise, students are asked to whom they might write a letter that would stand as a public affirmation of one of the ten values. Time is provided for those who actually want to write the letter. Students should keep copies of the letters sent, along with the replies.

TELEGRAM

The teacher passes out telegram blanks and explains

the per word rates for telegrams and night letters. Students are then asked to write a telegram or night letter to some prominent person about something which is important to them. After the telegrams are written they may be read in the small groups or to the entire class. The teacher helps the students to send the telegrams.

POSTCARDS

The teacher asks each student to think of three people he knows personally who have made him feel good in some way, and to write them brief thank-you notes. Then the teacher distributes postcards and invites the students to copy the thank-you notes onto the postcards and send them.

VALUES AND VALUE-FREE EDUCATION

No education is value-free. Despite protestations to the contrary by administrators and teachers, traditional public education is laden with values. The division of the day into "work" and "play"; the differentiation between major subjects such as English and math, and minor subjects such as art and ethics; the segregation by age; the seating arrangements; the authority of the teacher; the very fact that students are set apart in a school rather than being in the larger community—all these things shout their makers' values at the student. Passivity, obedience to authority, industry (or the appearance of industry) are the values promoted by traditional schools.

Nor is the personal-growth approach value-free. However, the values of education for personal growth are explicit rather than implicit: the individual is of unquestionable worth; awareness is essential for identity; risk-taking and self-disclosure are necessary in interpersonal relations; and awareness of one's values and moving to make values and actions more congruent are vital. In short, the values of *Composition for Personal Growth* are values of knowing one's world and of taking charge of one's own life.

5

Personal Growth

THE ACT OF COMPOSITION engages the student in three growth-producing activities: reflection, clarification, and commitment. In taking pen in hand and addressing the blank page before him, the student is led to *reflect* upon the welter of unorganized experiences that make up his life. He is impelled to bring an order to them, choosing and arranging them to build his model of reality. As he orders his existence, he begins to see patterns, and preferences emerge; he begins to *clarify* and to understand his own desires and his own actions. And as he commits his world to writing, he *becomes committed* to himself. By composing his world and communicating his insights to others, the student develops as an individual.

LEARNING BY DOING

The key to the personal-growth approach is the choice of subject and the use of audience. A student should be writing because he wants to say something that he thinks is important to some person or persons of importance to him, and because he wants to achieve a particular effect or set of effects on his audience. Audience feedback and the writer's response to that feedback are crucial. But if the writer does not care about his subject or about the audience, then the feedback is meaningless. Witness the student who takes a hasty glance at the grade on his returned paper and does not bother to look at the teacher's corrections and comments. On the other hand, if the audience does not care enough about the writer or his subject, then it will not produce significant feedback.

PEER FEEDBACK

There are many reasons why peer feedback may be the most significant and effective form of feedback: 1. Multiple responses to a piece of writing make the feedback more impersonal and easier to heed. 2. When the group reacts with consensus, it establishes some objective, or generally held, judgments about the writing in question. 3. When there is a disagreement within the group, it becomes apparent which aspects involve subjective, individual value judgments. 4. It is easier for peers to be candid in their reactions than for the teacher, who is aware of his special relationship to the student and must respond on several planes simultaneously. 5. Students are more likely to respond to the writing of a peer primarily on his own terms, whereas the teacher is more apt to focus on aspects of style and technique. Thus the student can shrug off teacher feedback as a manifestation of the generation gap: "Adults don't understand." But when a peer misunderstands him on a matter of importance, the student will respond to that feedback by accommodation.

GROWTH THROUGH DISCUSSION

Discussion, a vital aspect of the personal-growth approach, stimulates both linguistic and social growth. In a discussion, the participants build on one another's sentence constructions. A conversation is a linguistic collaboration in which each party borrows the words and phrases of others, restructures and elaborates upon them, and introduces new material.

Behind this verbal collaboration is a mental collaboration, a meeting and fusion of minds. The participants in this mental collaboration are taking in the attitudes, ideas, and points of view of the others even if they openly disagree.[1] Thus, social growth, as well as linguistic growth, is promoted; for it is through the ability to take in another person's point of view, to empathize, that one moves away from egocentricity towards a concern for others.

In most cases, typical class discussion could be better described as a series of individual dialogues between the teacher and separate students. Growth-producing conversation rarely occurs. (In fact, the Flanders Interaction Analysis indicates that most often teachers monopolize a good part of the discussion time, with the remaining time being dominated by two or three students.) The physical arrangement of the classroom, with the teacher up front facing rows of desks, or at the open end of a horseshoe, or at the head of a table, telegraphs the message that the teacher is the most important figure and students can learn only, or at least best, from the teacher. This notion is underscored by the common technique wherein the teacher asks questions to which he knows the answers; the students bid for the teacher's approval by getting the right answer, and pay little heed to what other students say.

Of course, equalizing all the participants, as in a peer

---

1. For further discussion of linguistic growth through dialogue, see James Moffett, *Teaching the Universe of Discourse*, Boston: Houghton Mifflin Company, 1968, pp. 72-83.

group discussion, is no guarantee that growth-producing dialogue will occur. If the members of the group do not really engage each other, if they merely hear each other out and wait their turn to speak, then nothing much of educational value will occur. It is up to the teacher to see that the students engage in genuine dialogue, and to foster the habits of questioning, collaborating, and qualifying—habits which produce the give-and-take quality of good dialogue.

GROWTH THROUGH GROUP PROCESS

Research has shown that classroom groups with diffuse and informal patterns of friendship and influence have more positive attitudes toward learning than do groups that are more formal and rigidly structured. More students in the informal groups think of themselves as having high group status than in the formal groups. Students who perceive themselves to have high group status tend to have higher self-esteem and a more positive attitude toward school work, and generally apply their intellectual abilities better than students who do not have a high regard for their group status.[2]

AWARENESS AND GROWTH

Who am I? How am I perceived by others? What do I value? How do my actions reflect my values? These questions are central in adolescence—that period of life when startling body changes and mushrooming social activity turn the eyes inward. This is the period when self-con-

---

2. For further details see Richard A. and Patricia A. Schmuck, *Group Processes in the Classroom*, Dubuque, Iowa: William C. Brown Company Publishers, 1971.

sciousness can become morbid introspection and egocentricity. It is the period when a healthy self-awareness is crucial for personal and social growth.

Composition for Personal Growth focuses on these three overlapping and interrelated areas: identity, interpersonal relationships, and values into action. In the work in each of these areas, the initial phase is awareness: helping the young person to become more aware of his identity—of his patterns, preferences, influences, competencies, body; helping the young person to become more aware of what he does in his interpersonal relationships—how he affects others, what he needs from others; and helping the young person become more aware of his values and the degree to which his actions reflect his values. The previous chapters have been devoted to activities through which the student can become more aware of his own identity, his role in his interpersonal relations and his theoretical and actual values.

After awareness, the second phase is growth: helping the young person develop competencies and cope with unavoidable shortcomings; helping the young person to better relate to others—to influence and be influenced, to give and receive feedback, to collaborate, to listen; and helping the young person to make his actions more consistent with his values.

6

Implementing the "Composition for Personal Growth" Approach

THE PARADOX of the teacher's role is that he is far less significant than the student's peers in the affectional relationship, and far too significant as an authority figure—as parental surrogate, civic authority, and dispenser of grades. The student may respond to teacher feedback in ways which severely limit his learning to write. He may, for example, become engaged in an assessment of the teacher's likes and dislikes and write to please or, perversely, to displease. Or he may react by withholding himself, writing briefly and grudgingly.

To prevent students from relating to him merely as an authority figure, the teacher should avoid lecturing excessively and use an action-response approach to learning (sometimes called the trial-and-error approach). He does not try to prevent the learner from making mistakes. He does not preteach the lesson, pointing out all the possible problems and suggesting solutions. Rather, he allows the student to plunge into the assignment using all the resources available to him, making mistakes if he must, and using feedback to evaluate his work. Errors become a valuable learning tool. And the teacher becomes a helper, not a judge.

Most good teachers use a variety of methods in the classroom, changing styles and techniques to suit varying needs. To paraphrase Ecclesiastes, there is a time to lecture and a time to listen, a time to share knowledge and a time to withhold knowledge, a time to identify potential problems and a time to allow problems to identify themselves, a time to intervene and a time to refrain from intervention. All these are teaching.

Like all effective instruction, teaching for personal growth calls for a wide variety of pedagogical modes. It is a flexible approach, adaptable to a broad range of individual teacher preferences.

This section is not intended as a straitjacket, a rigid exposition of what the teacher should or should not do; rather, it is intended to offer help and information for the teacher's consideration, to be employed as he sees fit.

If it is the role of the teacher to create learning opportunities, then he must have an atmosphere in which he can help his students to use those opportunities. Nothing is more enervating than the disorder and confusion that result when there are goals, but there is a lack of discipline. But by discipline we do not mean regimentation and autocratic rule. What we have in mind is that discipline which comes from establishing priorities of needs, and mutually acceptable ground rules for meeting those needs. Thus, while the teacher must remain non-judgmental and non-authoritarian in regard to the values expressed by his students, he must also help to establish and maintain behavior patterns which contribute to the class sense of vitality and purpose.

To create an atmosphere that is open, honest, and trusting, the teacher must himself be open, honest, and trusting. He needs to initiate but not to intrude, to be authoritative without being authoritarian. In short, the teacher must be responsible that learning takes place in his class, and not merely for covering the material or maintaining order.

GETTING STARTED

For teachers who have never used the workshop approach, breaking the class down into independent discussion groups can seem fraught with potential dangers. Will the students all follow instructions? Are they going to horse around? Won't they just sit around and gossip? How can I control the class when they're spread out doing different things? Most teachers find that these problems do not arise; in fact, students who are newly exposed to the workshop approach usually respond in a surprisingly responsible and serious manner.

There are two keys to success in introducing the workshop approach. The first is the teacher's commitment—he must show by his actions that he has faith in his students and in the approach. The second is the use of engaging activities which the student sees as relevant to his life (a rank-order problem or a forced-choice game is usually a good place to start).

This is not to say that there won't be problems. New behaviors for the workshop approach must be learned through practice, and many of the traditional schooling patterns must be unlearned. Students must learn to value the teacher in new ways: not as an authority figure to be obeyed or deceived, but as a helper to be used when needed; not as a font of wisdom, but as an organizer of activities and a resource person with special skills and useful information.

The students must learn to value other students in new ways: not as competitors for the teacher's attention and approval, but as sharers of experience; not as obstacles to the teacher's flow of wisdom, but as persons who can contribute additional perspectives to the understanding of life.

And finally, the student must learn to value learning in a new way: not as an acquisition of facts and a preparation for some indistinct future goal, but as a process of discovering, knowing, and evaluating himself and the universe.

COMMUNITY BUILDING

Some teachers worry about time "wasted" in class as students get to know each other and as the teacher gets to know the students. Yet several studies of classroom learning indicate that a feeling of group cohesiveness stimulates academic performance and fosters a positive attitude toward school. Many of the activities in *Composition for Personal Growth* promote this kind of community. Following are some specific activities which can be used at the start of a new year or term, when students are more or less strangers to each other. The teacher should clearly indicate to the students the importance of getting to know each other.

NAME TAGS

Besides enabling students to call each other by name,

name tags can contain lots of interesting information. Distribute four-by-six file cards and short pieces of masking tape to hold the cards in place. Ask the students to write the name by which they wish to be called in the middle of the card, and choose three or four of the following things for them to write around the edges: the name of a historical figure whom you would like to emulate; an object in your home that you are proud of; three things that you love to do, all ending in *ing*; a character from a story, novel, movie, or TV whom you admire; your nomination for the next president of the United States or ruler of the world; two things you do well; the place you would most like to visit; the place you would most like to live in.

Note: This is a positive-focus activity. Avoid using items that might have negative connotations (e.g. one thing in your house that you would like to get rid of).

ADDRESS LIST

Publish a list of the names and addresses of all the students in the class and their telephone number and birthdays. This will help the class to communicate with each other, to do things together outside the artificial world of the classroom.

SINGING SAM

This is a mnemonic device for helping students learn each others' names quickly. The class is seated in a circle. The first student will introduce himself by giving his name, preceded by an epithet that tells something he likes to do or is good at. For instance, "I'm Singing Sam." The next person says, "He's Singing Sam, I'm Knitting Barbara." This name-reciting proceeds around the circle, with each person calling off the names of all those who preceded him before adding his own epithet and name.

Note: This is not a contest; just a way to get to know names quickly. There is no penalty for not being able to recite all the names; when someone is stuck, anyone may help him.

ESTABLISHING RULES AND PROCEDURES

There is no one way to establish the type of open, yet ordered, classroom envisioned here. Some teachers will plunge right in; others will proceed in slow, deliberate steps. Some teachers are able to communicate a sense of order and purpose almost magically, and at the same time they have an intuitive awareness of what the class is feeling; others will need to clarify and restate, to consult with the class and to retrace and replan.

Here are some specific ideas for establishing rules and procedures, to be used when and if the need arises. Throughout the mechanics of establishing and maintaining rules and procedures, it is important for the teacher to reaffirm that he is not abdicating his responsibility to the students. The teacher's responsibility to his students should, in fact, undergo continual definition both by himself and by the students. This will undoubtedly be one of the underlying or explicit themes of the class meeting, described below.

THE CLASS MEETING

The class meets as a whole, with chairs moved into a tight circle. The teacher should sit as a member of the circle, not in a power position in front of the group or behind a big desk. Anyone may moderate. (If class meetings are held regularly, each student can have a turn acting as moderator.) The object of the meeting is to reach consensus on priorities, rules, and other matters concerning the entire class. Decisions should also be made about how the procedures and rules will be enforced.

SMALL GROUPS AND CLASS MEETING

The class divides into groups of four or five (see *Methods for Movement* below) to discuss and make recommendations about rules, procedures, and problems. It is important that the group's task be concrete, and that the discussion have a definite time limit. All groups can work on the same task, or tasks can be divided among the groups. Subsequently, the class meets as a whole to discuss and act upon the recommendations of the small groups.

TASK FORCE ON RULES AND PROCEDURES

A six-member task force is set up with staggered membership. The teacher can work out with the class a rotating system that will enable each student to serve a six-week term.

The task force can meet during class time to discuss class rules and procedures and can report to the class at a weekly meeting.

METHODS FOR MOVEMENT

Here are some ways for dividing a class into small groups for the activities outlined in this book:

COUNTING OFF

Decide how many students you want to be in each group (e.g. 5). Divide the total number of students in the class by this number (e.g. 35 ÷ 5). Then ask the students to count off by this quotient (e.g. 7). After each student has a number, have all the ones, twos, threes, etc., group together. Help move the chairs or desks so that each group forms a circle. Try to avoid having one person partially behind another or too far from the others for intimate conversation.

Counting off is a useful method when you want to arrange students into random groups.

PAIRS AND FOURS

Ask each student to go to someone that he doesn't know very well; this pair then picks another pair that they mutually agree upon. The foursome then finds a place to form a small circle for discussion. If there is a pair left over, they can join one of the foursomes, or each of the two can join a separate group making two fivesomes.

As a variation, each student in the class may be asked to pair off with a close friend, and then the pair find another pair that they don't know well.

CHOOSING AND CHOSEN

As a follow-up to PAIRS AND FOURS, ask the students to reflect on their habits of choosing and being chosen—do they as individuals tend to do the choosing or wait to be chosen?

Ask the students to decide which they want to try this time, reminding them that they can try a new behavior if they wish. Those who have decided to be choosers stand up and each standee chooses a classmate who is still seated. This pair discusses the exercise and then picks another pair to form a group of four. (Or each pair can decide whether it wants to be chooser or chosen, and the exercise can be repeated for pairs.)

CORNERS

Label each of the four corners of the room with one of the following words: Dominator, Wallflower, Joker, Griper. Ask each student to choose the word that best characterizes his behavior in groups and to move to that corner. There he should pair off with someone he doesn't know well, and then the two of them should find a pair from another corner. Or each corner can stay together as a group.

Other labels can be used for the corners; for example, to reflect interests or preferences: flavors of ice cream, colors, names of rock groups, sports.

GROUP YOURSELVES

Simply give instructions such as: "Form into groups of five by finding other individuals whom you want to know better," or, "Form into groups of four with people that you don't know very well." Before going on to the activity at hand, ask the small groups to discuss the feelings, the decisions, and the activity that marked the grouping process.

CROSS-FERTILIZATION

To recombine small groups, ask each group to count off within itself. Then all the new number ones meet, all the new twos, etc. Or the teacher could give instructions such as, "Each one find three people whom you haven't been with yet today," and proceed as in the Group Yourselves method above.

While the students are forming small groups, the teacher should be alert for special problems that might arise. Some students may fail to understand instructions and need clarification; others may find themselves left out as groups are formed and may need the teacher's help. The teacher may need to help with the seating arrangements.

DEVELOPING LISTENING SKILLS

Although listening to other students tends to be undervalued in a traditional, teacher-oriented classroom, it is crucial to a workshop classroom. Here are some specific methods for improving listening skills:

CLASS-MEETING AWARENESS

At the class meeting, the teacher asks students to be aware of the degree to which they listen to each other by noting such signs of not listening as cutting off another speaker before you are sure that he has finished, or changing the subject abruptly without acknowledging the ideas of the previous speaker.

CLASS MEETING WITH PROCESS OBSERVER

The teacher and/or one or two students serve as an observer at the class meeting. The observer may break in and interrupt the meeting whenever he sees that one speaker has apparently not listened to another.

FISHBOWLING

The class is divided into an inner circle of ten and an outer circle of twenty (a ratio of 1:2). Every member of the inner circle is to be observed by two members of the outer circle. The inner circle then holds a discussion; for example, Planning a Party, or Catalog Buying. After the discussion, each inner-circle member meets with his two outer-circle observers to see how well he listened and how well he was listened to. (Or, there is a general discussion of the listening that took place.)

The activity is repeated twice with different discussion

topics. The inner-circle membership is changed twice, so that all will have had a chance to be in the inner circle once and observers twice.

FISHBOWLING WITH PROCESS OBSERVER

Fishbowling occurs as in the last exercise, except that the teacher or some of the students act as process observers who comment on the meeting of the inner circle as it proceeds. e.g. "I'm seeing two or three people monopolize the discussion time." "Susan offered an idea that no one acknowledged." "John, I don't think you answered the question that Mary asked, let's listen to it again."

LISTENING TRIADS

The class is broken into groups of three. Members One and Two hold a discussion, e.g. about a rank-order problem, each trying to persuade the other to change his rankings. Member Three observes. After Member One makes his statement, Member Two must restate Member One's ideas to the satisfaction of Member One and the observer. Then Member Two states his ideas, and Member One must restate them before he can reply. The activity is repeated three times with different rank-order problems and members rotate so that each has a turn being observer.

ACKNOWLEDGEMENT

For practicing listening skills in either the class meeting or in the small groupings, a rule may be invoked which requires each speaker to comment upon the merits of the previous speaker's ideas before going on to present his own ideas.

DEVELOPING REFLECTION PATTERNS

Reflection is a necessary and vital activity for any learner, but schools seldom provide time or encouragement for it. Here are some specific teacher behaviors which will encourage reflection:

TWO MINUTES FOR REFLECTION

The teacher announces that before beginning to discuss a particular topic, he would like everybody to spend two minutes thinking about it, deciding what is important, and what they might want to say. The students may make notes if they wish. Two minutes is a very long time for a class to keep silent, but if the teacher shows that it is a time for serious thought, many of the students will use the time to good advantage.

"LET'S HEAR FROM THE OTHERS"

Often in a class discussion, a few students will dominate the conversation. After they have had a reasonable chance to speak, the teacher can break in and say, "Let's reserve the next five or ten minutes to hear from people who haven't yet spoken." This remark is usually greeted by a stony silence, but if the teacher is steadfast and allows the silence to continue, there is a good chance that some of the more reticent students will begin to speak up.

It is important to refrain from filling up what seems to be an embarrassing silence. The silence not only prods more members of the class into talking up, but it also encourages reflection.

THINK TANK

An area in the room is set aside for thinking only. Students can come here to sit and think—daydream, even.

Not to be confused with a reading corner or a discussion corner, the Think Tank gives respectability to thinking independently, an activity which is often frowned upon in school.

CLARIFYING RESPONSES[1]

Clarifying responses are short, probing questions which teachers can use to stimulate individual students to reflect further upon their values and attitudes. They are generally used when a student has expressed an interest in an activity or an idea. The accent is on the positive, on how to make a positive feeling clearer. For example, if the student says, "I'm going out for the baseball team this spring," the teacher may respond, "Do you enjoy playing baseball?" Thus he gives the student an opportunity to reflect on his choice, to see what aspect of "going out for baseball" is really important to him. The conversation might end at that point, but the student may allow the teacher's response to provoke him into some additional thinking about his life—what he chooses, what he likes, what he does.

The following is a list of sample clarifying responses.

1. Is that something you enjoy doing?

2. Are you glad about that?

3. How did you feel when that happened?

4. Have you considered alternatives?

5. Did you choose this?

6. Can you give me an example?

---

1. For a more detailed discussion of clarifying responses, see Raths, L., Harmin, M., and Simon, S. B., *Values and Teaching*, Chapter V., Columbus, Ohio: Charles E. Merrill Pub. Co., 1966.

7. Where would that lead?
8. What are some of the good things about that?
9. What other possibilities are there?
10. Do you do this often?
11. Would you like to tell others about it?
12. Would you do the same thing again?
13. How do you know it's right?
14. Do you think people will always believe that?

Reminders to the teacher in using clarifying responses:

Be nonjudgmental.

Keep the conference brief and directed at individuals (although others may be present).

Keep the *you* focus.

Stick to *how* questions—not *why* questions.

Watch out for negative situations: "Is that something that you enjoy doing?" is a killer statement to a boy who has just broken a window with a snowball.

TROUBLESHOOTING

Teaching and learning in a workshop classroom require skill and practice for both the teacher and the students. Although teachers are usually surprised at how willingly and ably students adapt to the workshop situation, difficulties sometimes arise. Following are some hypothetical problems, with suggestions for coping with them:

SILLINESS, HORSING AROUND

Teacher addresses the group or groups in the following way: "I see that you are unwilling or unable to carry out this activity. I would like you to think for a minute about whether this is because the activity touches you too deeply and personally to share with each other, or whether you find this activity irrelevant. Or is there some other reason?"

After the class has had a minute for reflection, the question is thrown open for discussion. Revisions in the activity can be discussed, as well as the advantages and disadvantages of sharing, risk-taking, and self-disclosure.

"THIS IS STUPID"

When one or two people in a group begin to make comments like, "This is stupid," or "What's the point of doing this?" the teacher can respond very much as suggested above. Or the teacher might consider this a good chance to discuss the nature of the program, or the emphasis of the particular exercise.

In the last analysis, however, the students are the best judges of what is irrelevant or stupid to them, and, if the group agrees with the few vocal ones, perhaps the activity should be discarded.

OFF THE SUBJECT

When the teacher perceives that one of the groups is wandering off the subject, he should wait to see whether the new subject seems to be relevant and important to the students—it may give him an idea for a new activity. If the new topic is meaningful and engaging to the students, the teacher might allow the discussion to continue, perhaps asking for a report to the class at the end of the meeting.

SMALL TALK

If the teacher believes the group has wandered off the subject and their conversation has degenerated into small talk, he might check this observation out with the group. Perhaps what may seem small talk to him may be of vital interest to the students. If the group agrees that they are off the subject and their talk is indeed small, the teacher could probe into their reasons for dropping the subject, as in the silliness problem. If the students believe that their conversation is important, the teacher might allow them to continue their discussion and report to the class at the end.

ONE GROUP FINISHED

When the teacher notices that one of the groups has finished the activity and is aimless while the others are still engaged, he may suggest a variety of things to them:

First, he could propose that they start another activity, such as a rank-order problem.

Second, he might ask them to devise an activity similar to the one just completed, which the class could later try.

Third, he could ask them to do some follow-up activities in their journals (e.g. "I Learned . . ." statements).

Fourth, he might invite them to use some of the open classroom activities, such as the letter-writing center, the card-sort piles, or the bulletin board.

Finally, he could ask them to suggest their own way to use the time available to them.

ONE GROUP TOO INVOLVED

When one group is avidly involved in an activity while all the other groups are ready to move on, perhaps the best course of action is to allow them to remain with that activity while the rest of the class goes ahead. When they are ready to join the class, the teacher can give the instructions to them separately. The teacher should remember that the activities themselves are never as important as the conversations they produce.

If the teacher feels that it is advisable to move the group along to the next activity, he can introduce the concept of unfinished business. A time slot can be assigned when anyone who so desires can finish activities or projects left undone, whether individually or in groups.

ESTABLISHING SUPPORT GROUPS

After the class has had practice working in small groups, support groups should be established. These are semi-permanent bodies which remain intact for a semester or longer, and enable the group members to form a more intimate, trusting relationship with some of their peers. Although other groupings are still used for most of the values activities, the support groups should meet several times a week for other planned activities.

Support groups generally work best with five or six members. Procedures for establishing support groups should be discussed at the class meeting. No matter how the selecting of group members may be handled, it should be done openly—every member of the class should have a chance to make his ideas and feelings known.

One method of selection is to have the students negotiate with each other to form pairs during a class meeting. That is, one student might say, "I would like to be in the same group as X." Then X would say if that was all right with him, or if he had a strong preference for another partner.

After all students are paired, the process is repeated to combine pairs into fours, fours into sixes. This process can be excruciatingly slow, or it may go very quickly.

The students may have some ideas of their own for building the support groups.

If the class is small, or cohesive enough, the small groups formed for a specific activity may, in a sense, be considered support groups, and these small groups can meet for two or three days running.

CAVEATS

Here are some common pitfalls for teachers to beware:

1. *Ultimatums:* "If you can't handle this responsibility, I will have to . . ." Whatever the ultimatum is, some student will force you to follow through or to retract your words. Ultimatums generally boomerang, creating more problems than they solve.

2. *Killer Statements:* "I should have known better than to expect you to be able to do this." There is no better way to alienate the class from the teacher.

3. *Nicknames:* "Knuckle Head" and "Wise Guy" are obviously damaging. Not so obvious, but possibly more damaging, are "Skinny," "Freckles," or even "Red." It is very hard to know what students may think about their nicknames; better avoid using them.

4. *Answering Your Own Questions:* Teachers sometimes fall into the habit of asking a question, and if there

is not an immediate response, they answer the question themselves in order to keep the class moving. Students often need time to reflect and compose an answer. The fact that they are silent does not always mean that they are bored or ignorant. Once the teacher falls into the habit of answering his own questions, the students soon learn to wait for his answer rather than think on their own.

5. *Asking Double Questions:* In introducing a subject for discussion a teacher is often inclined to ask double or even multiple questions. This satisfies the teacher's need to open a wide area for discussion, but it leaves the student uncertain as to where to focus his attention. Thus the student spends much of his creative thinking energy trying to guess what question is really being asked, or which of the questions raised is most important. For example: "What's happening here? How does Hamlet feel toward his mother? What does he know or suspect about her relationship with Claudius?" (Often the use of *or* signals a double question.)

6. *"Guess What I'm Thinking Of":* The teacher asks a question and then waits for an answer that agrees with the one he has in mind, disregarding any other answer that might lead the class away from the path that he wants them to take. The students learn that creative thinking is less important than satisfying the teacher. Sometimes the teacher will accept an answer but say, "Well, that's right, but it's not quite it, it's more . . ." Then he will answer the question his own way, showing that what the students say isn't really very important.

7. *Introjectors:* "Don't you think . . .?" "You don't really believe that, do you?" "Wouldn't you agree that

...?" or "Don't we all feel...?" These questions indicate that the speaker's primary interest is in furthering his own views rather than accepting other people's values and ideas. By casting his statement as a question which assumes a positive answer, the teacher can produce passive agreement, and underlying resentment.

8. *Playing to Win:* The attitude that there must be a winner and a loser in every encounter is common in schools. So long as the teacher feels that *he* must win or the student will—or that such a competition exists—the classroom will be a battleground.

9. *"I'll Do It Myself":* Many tasks are easy for teachers and difficult or awkward for students (running a class meeting, for example). These the teacher will often take on in order to avoid confusion, or to "get things moving." This kind of benevolent protection fosters habits of dependence and non-involvement on the part of the student. One rule of thumb might be, "Does my taking over this task release my students for a more important activity?"

10. *Individually Directed Negative Criticism:* Recent research indicates that when negative criticism of behavior or work is necessary, it is best given to the whole class in terms of general things-to-watch-out-for, rather than directed specifically to one individual.[2] Individually directed positive criticism, however, is beneficial so long as it is not given to the same one or two people all the time.

---

2. Schmuck, R. and P. *Group Processes in the Classroom,* Dubuque, Iowa: Wm. C. Brown Co., 1971.

SPECIAL CAUTIONS FOR USING PERSONAL-GROWTH ACTIVITIES

1. *Overscheduling:* Crowding too much into any one class period should be avoided. Nothing is more frustrating than being interrupted in the middle of a good discussion, or being rushed away from a subject one is very much interested in, by a bell. Plans should always allow for revision to accommodate to more (or less) interest and/or discussion than had been anticipated.

2. *Being in on Everything:* Naturally the teacher wants to know what is going on in the classroom, but too much attention, especially to small group discussions, can create an undesirable dependence upon the teacher. Given the opportunity, students will learn how to hold fruitful conversations among themselves, but if the teacher constantly circulates from one group to another, they are apt to get the impression that they need the teacher's leadership. The teacher should feel free to sit in on discussions, but should make it a habit to withdraw completely from time to time.

3. *Hidden-Purpose Strategizing:* The success of the personal-growth program depends in large measure upon complete openness of communication between teacher and students. The teacher should make the aims of the program clear from the beginning, and should remember to introduce every activity with a statement of purpose or general focus. There should be no having to guess why a thing is being done.

4. *Channeling Discussion to Own Agenda:* Every teacher will have his own ideas as to what points are important in a given discussion. It is essential to this

program, however, that class discussions not be thinly veiled lectures. If students are to develop the ability to think, talk, and write rationally, they must be allowed the freedom to find their own way even at the risk of going astray. And it is they who must judge what aspects of a given subject are relevant to their lives.

5. *Using Threatening Activities:* It is of utmost importance to avoid asking students to share personal concerns with strangers. Adequate time, and many experiences with community-building activities, should be provided before scheduling activities which call for sharing personal feelings or ideas. It is also important to avoid using threatening activities as attention-getting devices (e.g. choose someone in this class for whom you feel resentment). Many students have been conditioned to discredit what is pleasurable in school. They may react to the positive focus activities with flippancy or contempt. The teacher must, however, resist the temptation to snap them to attention with an anxiety-producing activity.

6. *Flexibility:* Flexibility is a requirement for both the *Composition for Personal Growth* program and the participants. The teacher should feel free to invent additional activities when the need arises. There is nothing sacred about the activities in this book, or about the order in which they appear. Students should have opportunities for nondirected private and/or public writing fairly frequently, though classes will differ in their needs and desires. If a class or a group wants to do some more structured public writing, such as composing a short story, they should certainly be encouraged, but as with other aspects of this program, it should not be graded or judged competitively.

7. *Conventional Expectations:* The first obstacles the teacher of *Composition for Personal Growth* is likely to encounter are the conventional expectations of his students. They are apt to look askance at activities that are not unpleasant, that don't involve rote memorization, that tie in with their lives outside of school. Many parents, too, are inclined to be suspicious of courses that fail to produce visible homework or grades.

Explaining the goals of the program—as often and in as much detail as necessary—along with the experience of the program itself should eventually solve the problem, but hard-core skeptics have remarkable persistence. And one cannot realistically expect that the merit of the program will be proved by miraculous behavior changes. Any change in attitude takes considerable time to be manifested in action, and the amount of time a student spends in personal-growth activities is minute in comparison with the accumulated time he has spent, and is currently spending, in conventional schooling. Personal growth does not take place overnight, and it may be months, or even years, before the full impact of a program such as *Composition for Personal Growth* can be recognized.

8. *Grading:* A competitive grading system is anathema to the learning environment advocated here. The competitive and individualistic values implicit in the traditional grading system are opposed to the values of collaboration and interdependence fostered by *Composition for Personal Growth*. If the school, the students, or the teacher require grades of some sort, plans must be carefully—and cooperatively—made so that all parties understand what work is to be graded and what the

criteria for evaluation will be. If possible, this should be done on an individualized basis. However, ideally, grading should be eliminated completely. For an account of the impact of grading on students and schools, see *Wad-Ja-Get? The Grading Game in American Education*[3] by Howard Kirschenbaum, Sidney B. Simon, and Rodney W. Napier, especially the annotated bibliography of research findings on the effects of grading.

TECHNICAL SKILLS FOR TEACHERS OF COMPOSITION

While this chapter has placed heavy emphasis on the teacher's ability to facilitate group processes, it is also necessary that he develop his skills and knowledge in teaching language. Semantics, rhetoric, transformational grammar, linguistic theory and history, communication media, and common usage are all important—not as "subjects" to be taught directly (except as the students' interests dictate), but as tools to help identify and clarify oral and written problems. Chapter IX contains suggestions for readings in these areas.

---

3. Kirschenbaum, H., Simon, S. B., Napier, R. W., *Wad-Ja-Get? The Grading Game in American Education*, New York: Hart Publishing Co., 1971.

7

General Techniques and Activities

IT IS DIFFICULT at first to know how long an activity will take, and thus how to plan for a whole class. Generally it is wise to allow plenty of time for each activity, but to have contingency activities just in case.

Teachers often suffer from a compulsion to fill up the entire period, whether the activity is meaningful or not. Nothing is more artificial. When the end of productive work has come, the teacher should not be afraid to say to the class, "I think we've had enough for today. The period will end in .... minutes. You may talk to each other quietly, read a book, or write in your journals."

In planning for the class, the teacher should keep in mind questions such as the following:

What are my objectives? Generally, in the personal-growth approach several objectives will be worked on at one time, some more overtly than others. It is often helpful to delineate one or two primary objectives from the areas of Identity, Interpersonal Relations, or Values into Action. At the same time, the teacher should be aware that too close a focus on objectives may cause the class to miss some incidental learning—perhaps more important than the planned objectives of the day.

What activities are to be used? Enough time must be

allowed for both ongoing and self-contained activities. Necessary materials must be arranged for in advance for both.

Other Considerations: The teacher should ask himself:

Have I provided enough time and adequate stimulus for discussion, for writing?

Have I considered student desires and interests?

Will it be possible to change the plan if on-the-spot events indicate that other activities would be preferable?

A SAMPLE LESSON PLAN

LESSON PLAN   for _____ (date), _____

(period) _____ (teacher) _____ (class) _____

1. What are my objectives? (Consult sections on Identity, Interpersonal Relations, Values into Action.)

2. What activity/activities do I plan to use?

   A. Time for each?

   B. Special materials?

   C. Provision for discussion?

   D. Provision for writing?

3. Possible follow-up activities?

4. How does this lesson plan show an awareness of student concerns and interests?

5. How does it allow for student initiative?

6. General remarks:

EVALUATION

There are two general categories of evaluation—formative and summative. Formative evaluation is an ongoing process whereby the evaluator's reactions are fed back, noted, and acted upon, rapidly and continuously. The function of formative evaluation is to correct and to guide. The messages collected by the thermostat and sent to the heating system are frequently cited as examples of formative evaluation.

Summative evaluation occurs when an activity is over. It often functions more as a tool of public relations, or grading, than as a means of influencing the conduct of the activity or the learning of the participants. The unreturned final examination paper, for example, has little influence on activities related to the study of the Boxer Rebellion.

Many evaluations in schools are summative rather than formative, whether the evaluations be by teachers grading students or by students grading teachers. The entire notion of accountability when it takes the form of sealed envelopes handed in to the office seems ill-suited to fostering growth in either the receiver or the sender. The use of self-evaluation and student feedback as suggested here offers opportunities for the growth of all involved in the activities.

STUDENT FEEDBACK

Feedback is an absolutely essential ingredient in a program using *Composition for Personal Growth*. Feedback forms serve several purposes. They offer the student the opportunity to write a message to an audience that is both interested and subject to influence. For the teacher, feedback is an invaluable supplement to his own evaluation of his class's work. Further, by providing him with

---

FEEDBACK FORM

1. How satisfied were you with this week's sessions? (circle one)

    1   2   3   4   5   6   7

    very   very
    dissatisfied   satisfied

2. What do you consider the high point of the week's work?

3. What things gave you satisfaction?

4. What would make these sessions better?

5. What can the teacher do to make these sessions better?

6. What can you do yourself to make these sessions better?

7. What issues, concerns, or questions would you like to see raised in class next week?

8. Free comment/suggestions/questions/jokes/etc.

_____

NAME (optional)

Please use the back
if you need more space for any item.

time to think and write about it, student feedback is instrumental in making the learner responsible for his own learning.

Feedback forms should be used at least once a week to allow the teacher to check out his observations, and to remind the students of their responsibility and power in shaping the course of their learning.

Preferably the same time should be set aside for filling out feedback forms each week. At the next class meeting the teacher should summarize what the feedback forms showed to be the prevailing opinions and the minority opinions. After these are discussed, the teacher summarizes the suggestions and recommendations made and tells his class which ones he is willing to try.

THE RIGHT TO PASS

In all personal growth activities the right of any individual to pass, to withhold his thoughts and ideas, to refrain from participating must be respected and supported with dignity. The teacher, as group facilitator, is in a key position to foster the attitude that a pass represents a conscious act by an individual which must be respected by all.

The motives for passing are so varied, and often so complex, that group members should refrain from conjecture as to why an individual passes at any given moment. There are many reasons why someone might choose to pass. The passer might find the topic too deeply personal to share his thoughts. The topic might touch off inchoate memories which tie his tongue. He might feel that his thoughts are undefinable, or might be considered misleading, or have been expressed so often as to be trite.

He might feel that he is protecting someone else. Or he might be concentrating on the group process as an observer and be unwilling or unable to shift his focus. And, of course, he might be thinking of something entirely off the subject, or even be daydreaming. Whatever the reason, it is crucial for the teacher to establish the sanctity of the pass early in the program.

GENERAL ACTIVITIES

BRAINSTORMING

This is the classic problem-solving tool, designed to release the creative potential in individuals and groups. A question or a problem is posed (e.g. What would be a good school symbol? slogan? How can we raise money for class rings?) and the group shoots out suggestions as rapidly as they can think of them.

Rules for Brainstorming:

1. Defer evaluation—all ideas are welcome.
2. Strive for quantity rather than quality—the more items on the list, the better.
3. Encourage off-beat and far-out ideas—they may have a germ to build on.
4. Piggy-back, or build on one another's ideas—this activity is a team effort, not a competition.
5. Record every idea—at least by a key word or phrase.

Good brainstorming requires practice, and the above rules should be reviewed often. It is very easy to fall into the trap of evaluating ideas as they come along, but this is counter-productive. It cuts down on the flow of ideas, and often potentially useful ideas are left unsaid because of the threat of instant evaluation.

Brainstorming works best in small groups of from three to seven. One person should act as scribe, or a tape recorder may be used. Generally, a specific time limit, such as five or ten minutes, should be set.

At the end of the brainstorming session, the list of ideas can be read over. Evaluations may be made using spectrum analysis (see below).

SPECTRUM ANALYSIS

Often we dismiss an idea because we consider it faulty or unworkable. Nevertheless, the idea may have a germ which can be built on if it survives the initial negative responses. Spectrum analysis asks that critics look first at the good points of an idea before stating its weaknesses. Spectrum analysis can be used with brainstormed ideas or in any other problem-solving situation. A proposed solution is taken up, and the class lists the good points of the proposal. Next they list its weaknesses, and compare and evaluate which outbalances which.

ALTERNATIVES SEARCH

Human beings often operate within a fairly narrow range of behavior. The alternatives search is a brainstorming activity designed to expand the repertoire of possible courses of action for real or hypothetical situations.

A problem may be posed by a student or by the teacher. Possible solutions or courses of action can be brainstormed in small groups, and then shared by reading lists aloud or by posting them. If the problem is a real one, the individual who posed it can select some of the ideas as a self-contract.

Sample alternatives search questions:

1. How to send love to someone far away.
2. How to make Christmas more meaningful.
3. How to tell parents, "I love you, but leave me alone."
4. What to do about a friend who has a body odor problem.
5. How to get along with your brother or sister.
6. What to do when your best friend starts smoking marijuana and wants you to try it.
7. Ways to make money/save money.
8. Ways to spend Saturday night/Sunday afternoon.

SELF-CONTRACTING

A self-contract is often a very helpful device when an individual wants to work on solving a problem or effecting a change in his life. After the problem has been identified, and possible courses of action proposed through an alternatives search or through a group discussion, the individual chooses a feasible course of action and contracts with himself to follow that course. The group devises an objective method of evaluating how successfully the action has been carried out. The individual reports back to the group at the end of a week and his progress towards the objective is assessed.

For instance, a student states that his objective is to

reduce friction with his brother. He chooses the following course of action from among the proposals made in the alternatives search: "Find one good thing to say about him each day and say it at supper."

To evaluate the effectiveness of this course of action, the student might be asked to keep a record of the nice remarks he made to his brother, and of the number and type of disagreements they had during the week. The group will determine whether there has been any improvement in the student's relationship to his brother.

FORCE-FIELD ANALYSIS

A force-field analysis can be helpful in deciding whether or not to adopt a certain course of action, or in deciding between two conflicting courses of action. For example, a person is trying to decide whether or not to go to Florida for his Christmas vacation. He draws a line down the center of a piece of paper or on the blackboard and labels one side "Reasons to Go" and the other "Reasons Not to Go." Then he puts down all the reasons he can think of on each side. After making as exhaustive a list as possible, he might circle the most compelling reasons on each side. Now he is ready to weigh all the factors and come to a decision.

If two conflicting courses of action are involved, these are proposed on each half of the paper. For example: "Reasons for Going to College" and "Reasons for Joining the Army."

An individual can do a force-field analysis of his own problem. But a small discussion group or the whole class can often be helpful in generating the lists because they bring a variety of points-of-view to bear on the problem.

The force-field analysis technique can also be used

with hypothetical problems. Small group discussion of the relative merits of the factors involved can lead to significant value exploration and clarification. Here are some sample topics: Jill thinks that she is pregnant; should she or shouldn't she tell her mother? Should a young person take up smoking? Should you take the college prep or the general course? Should you cheat on the science exam?

One of the most important effects of the force-field analysis is that it exposes any discrepancy between a person's actions and his values. Listing side by side all the known forces restraining a person from acting, and all the known forces compelling him to act, clearly shows the individual what is holding him back from changing his life. He is more apt to try to make his values and actions more congruent.

The following example illustrates a force-field analysis:

VALUE: STOPPING SMOKING	
Forces restraining me from stopping	**Forces compelling me towards stopping**
I enjoy the smell and taste. It makes me more comfortable in a new situation. It's a social thing to offer cigarettes and to borrow them. Etc.	I am concerned over cancer and heart disease. It costs too much. My parents want me to stop. Etc.

RANK ORDER

Rank ordering can be a useful technique in stimulating discussion and bringing values and attitudes into focus. Participants are given three situations and are asked to rank them from the most desirable to the least desirable. For example:

Rank-Order Problem I: If your values conflicted with your parents' values, how would you rank these three courses of action from most desirable to least desirable:

- I would hide my conflicting values from my parents in order to avoid hurting them, even if this means doing things behind their backs.
- I would show my parents where I stand by my actions, even if it upsets them.
- I would bend enough to my parents' desires so that I might influence them to bend to mine, even though I would be complying with my parents only in order to manipulate them.

After the students rank order the three solutions and record them in their journals, small groups can compare and discuss their rankings. The groups can make lists of the three or four most compelling (or repelling) characteristics of each solution. There is no reason to attempt to achieve consensus on the rankings or on the lists or characteristics.

When the participants have spent a reasonable amount of time working on the three solutions, the teacher can ask each person to think of a fourth solution which would be more desirable than those on the original list. Their suggestions can then be rank-ordered and discussed.

Finally, the teacher can ask the participants to test their rankings against reality. They can note in their journals whether their top ranking reflects what actually happens. They can record what actions they have taken, or can take, to make their top ranking more consistent with reality. This might also be a good time for some "I Learned . . ." or "I Believe . . ." statements to be written in the journals.

Rank ordering may be supplemented by brainstorming, alternatives search, and role taking and role playing. In role taking, the participants are asked to rank the situations as they might if they were parents. In role playing, the participants are asked to play the part of one of their own parents and to rank and discuss the solutions as they think that parent might.

Rank-Order Problem II: As a good friend of someone who has developed bad breath, rank these three alternatives:

I would tell him.

I would send him an anonymous letter.

I wouldn't do anything, even when I hear others secretly making jokes about him and his breath.

After entries in journals and group discussion, additional alternatives can be brainstormed in groups. The lists are then read off, and students can add especially useful ideas to their journals.

Rank-Order Problem III: If you were the parent of a seventeen-year-old daughter, how would you rank these three situations from most desirable to least desirable (role *taking*):

You discover that she has the reputation of being promiscuous.

You are informed by the local police that she has been booked on a marijuana-use charge.

She tells you that she is engaged to a person of another race.

After journal entries and small-group discussion, the leader can ask how the rankings might change if one of the conditions were changed. For instance, how might the ranking change if daughter were changed to son? Or if marijuana were changed to heroin? Or if drug-user were changed to drug-seller? Additional journal entries may be made, as well as "I Learned..." or "I Believe..." statements.

RANK ORDERS WITH ROLE PLAY

Each of the following exercises asks the participant to play the role of a specific person whom he knows well. These activities should be followed by small group discussions *in character* about the rankings. (Again, there is no need to try to reach consensus on either rankings or reasons.)

Problem I: Role play your own mother and rank the following, best to worse:

Your son/daughter (i.e. you) stays out until five A.M. on a Saturday night date.

Your son/daughter announces that he/she is dating a person of a different race.

Your son/daughter announces that he/she is going to drop out of school as soon as legally possible and get a job.

Problem II: Role play one of your brothers or sisters and rank order the following, best to worst:

Your brother/sister (i.e. you) borrows one of your favorite records and scratches it.

Your brother/sister (you) gets a better report card than you do and won't let your parents forget it.

Your brother/sister (you) picks a quarrel with you and your mother comes to take his/her side.

Problem III: Role play one of your teachers and rank-order the following situations, best to worst:

Your students do very well on the College Board exam in your subject.

Your students feel comfortable about asking for your advice and help with their personal problems.

One of your students who was shy, withdrawn, and filled with self-doubt at the beginning of the year is now much more outgoing, happy, and self-confident.

Think of a situation that you, role-playing teacher, would consider better than any of those listed.

Possible journal activities to follow these role-played rank orders include "I Learned . . ." statements, letters from the role-played character explaining the ranking, and dialogues between the role-played character and someone else about the rankings.

Reality testing can be carried out by asking the real individuals how they would rank the given items. Differences and similarities can then be entered in the journal.

In developing rank-order problems it is important to choose real issues and areas of genuine concern to the students. Rank-order problems involving concrete situations with realistic choices related to the issue seem to promote the best discussion. Students soon learn to make up very good rank-order problems.

As in all values-related activities, the teacher's own position on the rank-order problem is highly significant. He has to try to avoid being caught between the Scylla of imposing his own values on the students (even unintentionally), and the Charybdis of concealing his attitudes and appearing to take no firm stand on anything.

And it is equally important that he not be trapped in the quicksand of complete relativism, suggesting that everyone's opinion is equally valid; while at the same time, he must avoid using rank-order problems or any other value-clarifying activity to teach that one of the choices is the best or the right one. Any taint of such a hidden agenda would have a devastating effect on the openness of the students and on their willingness to explore their values.

Activities to Expand Rank-Order Problems:

1. List the three most compelling (or repelling) characteristics of each alternative.
2. Think of a more desirable alternative to add to the list.
3. Test against reality (choices against behavior).
4. Formulate "I Learned . . ." or "I Believe . . ." statements.
5. Brainstorm to search for additional alternatives.
6. Change the variables and rank again.

7. Role take.

8. Role play.

ROLE PLAYING AND ROLE TAKING

In role playing an individual takes the part of another and tries to act and respond as he imagines that person would.

In role taking the individual responds and acts as he thinks he would or should if he himself were in the given situation. Role-playing and role-taking activities can vary from a simple situation eliciting a single word response, to a rank-order problem, to a complex problem drama with pre-planned scenario.

Role playing and role taking can serve many purposes:

1. To rehearse a potentially threatening situation, such as asking for a date, or telling your mother that you are pregnant.

2. To clarify ideas and values by exploring what one might do and say in a given situation.

3. To explore a problem situation, looking at alternative courses of action and their probable consequences. (This could follow an alternative search.)

4. To help understand how others might feel in a given situation; to increase one's power of empathy.

5. To observe patterns of behavior and to note how unique or how common are one's responses to a given situation.

Although role plays can last up to an hour or even longer, generally the briefer role plays, lasting from two to ten minutes, are more effective. Role plays don't necessarily build to a climax or conclusion, so it is best if the leader cuts the action when he thinks that enough data has been produced for analysis and discussion.

The discussion might focus on questions such as the following: What value issues have been raised? What attitudes have been revealed in the behavior of the participants? Was any of the behavior designed to conceal attitudes and feelings? ("I saw . . . , and I imagined . . ." statements might be useful in relation to these last two questions.) Did anything happen that couldn't really happen? What do you think were the feelings of the participants at certain points (to be checked with the participants)? How do you think the situation would develop from this point?

After the analysis and discussion, the role play can be continued, picking up again where it had stopped or at some other point (past or future); or another set of participants can replay the situation; or a new situation can be introduced.

Role playing and role taking can follow different formats:

Assigned Parts: The teacher asks for volunteers to play assigned parts in concrete situations: e.g. The roles: mother and son; the situation: the son has just come in at 4 A.M. on Sunday morning.

Chairs: One person takes both or all the parts, switching from chair to chair as he switches characters. This technique can also be used to represent different facets within the personality: e.g. Cautious Jane and Carefree Jane have a discussion about whether or not to go to

Fort Lauderdale for the spring vacation.

Teams: When the situation is potentially too risky for individuals to play a role, chairs can be set out to represent imaginary players, and decisions as to what they say and do can be made by teams: e.g. Jack is bored at the dance and wants to go for a little ride. What does Jill, his date, do, and what happens from there? A team of boys decides on Jack's actions and speech, a team of girls decides on Jill's (or vice-versa).

Telephone: To demonstrate the difference between communicating with and without the aid of body language, the role players sit in chairs back-to-back. The onlookers can see both, but the players must rely on voice alone.

Problem Drama: If a member of the group has a problem which he feels he would like to discuss, problem drama can clarify the problem and help find alternative solutions: e.g. If Fred is constantly fighting with his mother, he might try to explain what generally goes on, and give an example of a situation which might set off a fight. Then he could play his mother, while other members of the group take the parts of Fred and other members of the family. Or the real Fred could observe as others in the group take all the parts.

Street Theater: This is perhaps the most intriguing use of role playing, and it is one method of translating values into actions by an act of public affirmation. Parades and picket lines are examples of street theater; the mock search-and-destroy mission staged at the Capitol by the Vietnam Veterans Against the War was a fanciful use of street theater attempting to affect the consciousness of others. And Hamlet used a variation of street theater in his play within a play, where his avowed purpose was to "catch the conscience of the king."

REVEALED DIFFERENCES SURVEY

The revealed-differences survey is used to discover which of an individual's attitudes, beliefs, and feelings are common, and which are unique. It also indicates how an individual's perception of the attitudes, beliefs, and feelings of others squares with reality.

For example, the teacher may ask: How many dates should a boy and girl have before it is proper for the boy to kiss the girl goodnight? The teacher asks each student to write down on a piece of paper the number of the date and to indicate whether he is a boy or a girl. While the papers are being collected, the teacher suggests that each student write down for his own use an estimate of what the most common answer will be for boys, and what the most common answer will be for girls. (Later on, students might also like to estimate the variance, that is, the spread from the lowest vote to the highest vote.) The votes can quickly be tallied on the blackboard:

answer choices →

	1st	2nd	3rd	4th	5th	6th	7th	8th
BOYS	𝍦 𝍦	///	//	/		/		
GIRLS	//	///	////	////		/	/	

Suggestions for other questions: How much money do you spend on clothes per year? How much allowance should you receive? How late are you allowed to stay out on Saturday night? How late should you be allowed

GENERAL TECHNIQUES AND ACTIVITIES [123

to stay out on Saturday night? How often do you go to church? How many hours of television do you watch a week? How much money do you expect to be earning in ten years? Do you drink alcoholic beverages: never, seldom, occasionally, frequently, regularly?

CONTINUUMS, PERCENTAGE PROBLEMS, LIKERT SCALES:

Most value problems are not either/or situations. *Continuums, Percentage Problems,* and *Likert Scales* can be used to break down the oversimplified thinking which splits people into two diametrically opposed camps.

Continuums: Draw a horizontal line on the blackboard. Choose one particular issue or attitude. Label the two endpoints and the middle of the line to represent polar and middle-of-the-road positions. For example, at one end you might write: Eager Egbert—the super-patriot who is so committed to the military that he would do anything to enlist—lie about his age, sell his mother. At the other end you would write: Maiming Malcolm, who would shoot off his toes rather than face military service. Between these two extreme positions lies a wide range of value positions. The exact center is marked "Compulsively Moderate Campbell" to help people move off the fence. Each person places a check somewhere along the line to indicate where he stands on the issue:

|—————————————————+—————————————————|

| Eager | Compulsively | Maiming |
| Egbert | Moderate Campbell | Malcolm |

Other continuum issues include:

    Complete Racial Separation—Forced Interracial
        Marriage;

Never Tell the Truth—Never Lie;

Ban All Cigarettes—Give Out Free Cigarettes to All Children.

The Likert Scale: The Likert Scale is similar to the continuum, except that several clearly defined positions (usually five or seven) are identified. For example: How do you value premarital chastity in your marriage partner?

1	2	3	4	5
Absolutely essential	Highly desirable	Some consideration	Minor consideration	Irrelevant

How strict should teachers be in class?

1	2	3	4	5
Very firm	Firm	Firm in some situations; liberal in others	Allow children some voice in class rules and procedures	Let children do whatever they please

The Likert Scale can be used with the Revealed Differences Survey to show the range of differences or the degree of agreement within a class or among several classes.

Percentage Problems: A question is posed, and students indicate where they stand on a line marked off on a percentage scale.

```
. . . . . . . . . . .
─────────────────────────────
0  10  20  30  40  50  60  70  80  90  100
```

.	.	.	.	.
0	25	50	75	100

e.g. What percent of the defects in your bicycle, car or house would you reveal to a potential buyer? What percent of your personal life do you share with your mother? Your brother? What percent of the homework assigned do you do? What percent of your free time do you spend watching television?

Revealed Differences Surveys may be used along with Percentage Problems.

THE FOUR CORNERS GAME[1]

The teacher posts response words or numbers in the four corners of the room. A question is asked orally, and/or dittoed or written on the blackboard.

The teacher gives the following directions: "Listen carefully to the question. There is a word posted in each corner of the room. Choose the word which corresponds to your answer to the question, and then go to that corner." (If numbers are used, the choice of words should be posted on the blackboard or dittoed.)

Sample questions and alternative answers:

1. How do you react when you're asked a question in class and don't know the answer?

    a. Con-artist
    b. Honest John
    c. Shame-faced Sam
    d. Laughing Larry

2. How do you feel when someone else is unjustly punished?

1. Adapted from a suggestion by Marge Feltonic.

    a. Silently angry
    b. Calm, unconcerned
    c. Confused
    d. Righteous Avenger
3. How do you feel about being corrected by the teacher?
    a. Angry
    b. Grateful
    c. Embarrassed
    d. Threatened
4. How do you feel about being corrected by peers?
    a. Stupid
    b. Unliked
    c. Pleased
    d. Hurt
5. How do you feel toward a teacher's pet?
    a. Jealous
    b. Admiring
    c. Indifferent
    d. Antagonistic
6. How does a permissive teacher make you feel?
    a. Thrilled
    b. Insecure
    c. Disappointed, cheated
    d. Puzzled
7. What is your attitude towards a friend who has wronged you?
    a. Infuriated (extremely angry)

b. Compassionate (full of pity)
c. Revengeful (wanting to get even)
d. Nonchalant (not caring)

8. How do you feel about doing chores at home?
    a. Jubilant (very happy)
    b. Resentful (full of anger)
    c. Resigned (submitting calmly)
    d. Arrogant (self-important, haughty)

9. What is your attitude toward strict parental control?
    a. Rebellious (fighting back)
    b. Submissive (obedient)
    c. Oppressed (burdened)
    d. Secure (protected)

10. What is your attitude toward death?
    a. Terrorized (fearful)
    b. Dubious (uncertain)
    c. Apathetic (not caring)
    d. Elated (happy)

11. How do you feel when you are with contemporaries who are strangers to you?
    a. Nonchalant
    b. Alienated
    c. Aggressive
    d. Reticent

12. How do you act in a group of your parents' contemporaries?
    a. Intimidated

            b. Taciturn
            c. Supercilious
            d. Unctuous
13. How do you respond to being kidded by peers?
            a. By counterattacking
            b. By acting fragile
            c. Condescendingly
            d. Apathetically

"I LEARNED..." STATEMENTS

This activity is used as a follow-up to generate written reflection and clarification after some other activity in this program has been completed. After a rank-order problem, for instance, participants are asked to write three to five or more "I Learned..." statements in their journals.

An "I Learned..." statement begins in one of the following ways:

"I learned that I..."

"I re-learned that I..."

"I discovered that I..."

"I noticed that I..."

"I realized that I..."

The second *I* is important because the purpose is to focus on the self and on what was learned about oneself from the preceding activity. For instance, "I learned that all people are different" is not as useful as "I learned that I often forget how different people are."

When recording "I Learned . . ." statements in the journal it is helpful to identify the activity that stimulated them. Here is an example of a journal entry for "I Learned . . ." Statements:

After a rank-order discussion about conflict between parents and young persons:

1. I learned that I often try to manipulate my parents even though I don't like them to manipulate me.

2. I discovered that I don't really have as many conflicts with my parents as some of my friends.

3. I noticed that I sometimes don't say what I feel because I'm afraid that others will laugh at me, and then somebody else says the exact same thing and nobody laughs.

"I BELIEVE . . ." STATEMENTS AND ACTION TESTING

Here is another follow-up activity which can stimulate further clarification of some of the values and attitudes explored in other exercises. After an activity, such as a forced-choice game, participants are asked to write one or two or more "I Believe . . ." statements in their journals.

An "I Believe . . ." statement may begin as follows:

"I believe in . . ."

"I affirm . . ."

"I stand for . . ."

"I hold dear . . ."

As with "I Learned . . ." statements, the journal entries

should identify the activity which stimulated the statements.

If the teacher or class decide to follow up "I Believe . . ." statements with action testing, the participants are asked to write the answers to each of the following four questions for each "I Believe . . ." statement:

1. In what way can you publicly affirm this belief?

2. How can you act on this belief?

3. What patterns of action can you pursue to uphold this belief?

4. Are you doing or have you done any of the things in questions 1, 2, and 3?

SHARING "I LEARNED . . ." AND "I BELIEVE . . ." STATEMENTS

Occasionally it is effective for the teacher to ask volunteers to share their "I Learned . ." or "I Believe . . ." statements by reading them to the class. This gives the participants some idea of the range of responses, their commonalities and their differences. And for individuals, this creates an opportunity for risk taking and for public affirmation.

The teacher may prefer to set aside space on the bulletin board for "I Learned . . ." and "I Believe . . ." statements, signed and unsigned. No one should ever be forced to share.

HERE-AND-NOW WORDS, THEN-AND-THERE WORDS

At the beginning of class, or after a stressful situation, the teacher might ask the students to write the date and the exact time in their journals, and to write four separate words which express the feelings that they are having right here and right now. They then take one of those words and write one or two sentences explaining or expanding on the feeling.

Here is an example from my own experience: July 28, 1971, 5:28 P.M. Frustrated. Relieved. Tired. Pleased. I'm feeling pleased because I made myself write several difficult pages for the teacher's handbook today, despite the beautiful weather and the call of swimming and other summer pleasures.

Here-and-Now Words often raise to a conscious level feelings which are unconscious or repressed. When raised to the conscious level, feelings that are bothersome or nagging are acknowledged, and even if they cannot be dealt with any further at that time, the acknowledgment makes them less bothersome.

By reviewing a month's here-and-now entries in his journal, an individual can often discover what patterns of feelings underlie his behavior, and what feelings he consistently represses. He may also write some "I Learned..." statements.

Then-and-There Words can be used to help build the power of empathy. To use this technique, the teacher asks students to imagine what here-and-now words a character from literature or history or real life might have recorded at some given moment. (This employs role playing.) For example: Write four here-and-now words that Macbeth might have recorded to describe his feelings when he saw the woods begin to move. If you had been in that particular situation, what would your here-and-now words have been? (This employs role taking.)

INVENTORIES

Inventories can be used to help individuals see patterns and preferences operating in their own lives. They also illustrate degrees of individuality or conformity among people. Some inventories, such as *Twenty Things I Love To Do* are best kept private in the student's journal; others, such as *Possessions,* or *Heroes,* can be shared in small groups. "I Learned . . ." statements are often a useful follow-up activity.

Possessions: Participants are asked to record the answers to the following questions in their journals. Lists can be shared in small groups or read anonymously and guesses made as to the author's identity:

1. If your house were on fire, what two things would you grab on the way out (assuming your family and pets have all been removed)?

2. If you came home and found your house had been broken into and burgled, what two things would you look for first?

3. Name one item that you have in your wallet that reflects an achievement of yours.

4. If you were forced to leave your home and had to pack all your possessions in only one suitcase, what items would you choose?

5. What two of your things would you want to share with a very dear friend who is seriously ill in the hospital?

Success Symbols: Students record their answers in their journals, and lists may be shared as in *Possessions*:

1. What is one artifact of success which you have in your desk or room or home?

2. Do you have a photograph which marks a successful experience?
3. Describe an object which people notice when they come into your room.
4. Describe something in your home which you are proud of, but which you normally don't show to others.
5. What event do you have on your calendar that you are looking forward to with great anticipation?

Heroes and Others: Answers are recorded in journals, and lists may be shared.
List the following:

1. a fictional character whom you admire
2. a person from history whom you admire
3. a nationally known person, living now, whom you admire
4. a movie personality whom you would like to be like
5. a TV program that you would like to be on
6. a singer or other musician that you would like to sing or play like
7. an author that you would like to write like.

Pages for a Biography: Students write a journal entry on one of the following topics:

All the different hair styles I have worn

How I have spent my last five spring vacations

All the Christmas presents I can remember giving my mother

What I have done on New Year's Eve for the last five years

How I have celebrated my birthday the last five times

The last five times that I have cried

These pages can be shared in small groups, or turned in and read anonymously for the group to guess each author's identity.

Topical Inventories: Inventories can be made up for many topical situations. For instance, an interest in ecology could stimulate an inventory of electrical appliances we have in our house we could do without; or a log could be kept of a week's use of the family car; or a list made of all the non-recycled items used in one day.

"I SEE . . ." AND "I IMAGINE . . ."

This technique is very helpful in pointing up the difference between observations and judgments. One person describes an observed behavior in another; he then says what he imagines is the reason for the behavior. For example: "I see you smile, and I imagine that you are happy with the proceedings." Or, "I see you fold your arms and move back, and I imagine that you are bored with the activity and are withdrawing."

The person who has been observed may then validate the observation: "Yes, as a matter of fact, I don't see the point of this exercise," or "No, actually I was thinking about a joke I heard last night."

FANTASY

In these exercises the teacher leads the class through a mental exploration of their inner worlds. Generally the students will have their eyes closed. The teacher or student leader should try to use a quiet, image-evoking speaking manner, and he should allow time after each direction for the students to dwell with the experience in their minds.

After the fantasy, the teacher may ask for "I Learned . . ." statements, or for some form of dramatic monologue or role playing.

Here are some sample fantasy exercises:

Your Bedroom: As you stand in the hall outside the bedroom, is the door open or shut?—Go into the room. Go to the bed.—Is it made, or unmade, or in between?—What sort of cover is there on it?—Feel the texture of the cover.—Look under the bed; what's there?—Look at the walls; are there pictures or other decorations?—What kind of a person would have these things on his walls?—Go to the closet.—What kind of clothes are in the closet?—Look at the labels in the clothes.—Do they tell you anything about the person who wears them?—Look at the shoes.—Are they shined or not?—Are they in neat rows or scattered about? What do they tell you about the wearer?—Go to the dresser.—What things are on the top of the dresser—Look in the top drawer.—What does this show you about the owner?—Are there any books in the room?—What kind?—Are there magazines?—Records?—What else is worth noting in this room?

Activities: Write a report that a private detective might write if he were asked to gather information about you and visited your room during your absence.

Write a dialogue between a hippie and a hard hat who chance to be examining your room together.

How do you expect your room will change in five years? What is in your room now that was not there one year ago?

Ahab: Stand on your right leg for three minutes. If you wish you may rest your left knee on the chair, but do not let the foot touch the floor. Try to keep your eyes closed.

After three minutes: Now sit down, keeping your left foot from touching the floor. You have lost your left leg just below the knee. Think about the activities you have planned for this evening. How will you have to change them?—Picture yourself hobbling down a city street.— It starts to rain, a downpour.—How do you manage to get shelter?—You are on a subway.—Notice the eyes of the people sitting across from you.—What are they thinking?—Think of your career plans.—How will they have to be changed?—Think of three things you love to do.— How can you change your life so that you can do those things?

Activities: Write some "I Learned . . ." statements in your journal.

Write a letter to a friend telling him how you have had to alter your life since you lost the use of your left leg.

If your leg were to be restored for just one day, what would you do?

As the teacher reads over the fantasy again slowly, try to reconstruct your here-and-now feelings at each point and write them down.

Cocoon: Find a comfortable position. You are in a

lovely, soft, white cocoon.—You are resting before coming out to be in the world again. You are comfortable and at peace.—Feel the space and the softness about you.—Now you start to build an ideal place for yourself within the cocoon; you can make the space as large or as small as you want, and any shape you want.—Is there music in your cocoon?—What kind? What color are the walls? —They can be any color you want.—Are there pictures on the walls, or other decorations?—You may invite anyone you like into your cocoon, as many people as you like, or you can be alone.—You may have a window in your cocoon.—What scene do you want to have outside the window?—Is it a place you know, or is it an imaginary scene?—What furniture do you have in your cocoon? —Is there any food?—What kind?

Now, you have to slowly leave your cocoon and return to the world.—Is there something you want to bring back with you?—Reach out to touch it.—But the cocoon fades, slowly fades away as you gradually return.—When you are ready, open your eyes.

Activities: Spend the next ten minutes describing your cocoon in writing. What aspects of your cocoon do you think are unique? What aspects do you expect others will share? In what way does your cocoon reflect your personality and your life? Can you identify any specific influences which have led you to the choices you have made?

The cocoon descriptions may be read anonymously in small groups, and the group can try to guess the identity of each author.

CATALOG BUYING

Sears or other general mail order catalogs can be used

for a variety of activities; every classroom should have several.

Individual Buying: Students are asked to take ten minutes to decide how they would spend $100 buying from the catalog. They can enter their lists in their journals, and also share them with other members of the group.

They can then be asked to answer the following questions in their journals:

> What items would not have been on your list two years ago?
>
> What items probably will not be on your list two years from now?
>
> What do the items show about your wants and needs?
>
> What proportion of the items are for your private use, and what proportion can be shared with others?
>
> If the items include clothing, what influenced you to select a particular style? Which items would your parents approve and which would they disapprove?

Sometimes the lists may be collected and read aloud anonymously. Members of the group can try to guess who wrote each list, giving reasons for their guesses. After all the lists are read, authors identify their own lists.

Group Buying: The class is divided into groups of five and each group is given one catalog and asked to take twenty minutes to determine how it would spend $200.

After the lists have been completed, each student writes answers to the following questions in his journal:

1. How satisfied were you with the group's selections?
2. Did your group buy things for the benefit of the whole group, or did you split the money and buy individually?
3. How was this decision made, and what part did you play in it?
4. Who held the catalog?
5. Which items on the list were your idea?
6. Who wrote up the list, and how was he chosen?
7. If you were going to repeat this activity, what would you do differently?
8. Write one or two or more "I Learned . . ." statements connected with this exercise.

Group Buying with Fishbowling: One group is given a catalog and told to decide how to spend $200. The other students form a circle outside the buying group. Each person in the outer group chooses a person in the inner group to observe. After the buying decisions have been made, the observers confer with the observees. They discuss the questions listed above (*Group Buying*). They may also discuss other questions such as the following:

How active a part did you take in the decision-making?

Were you able to express your opinions?

How carefully did you listen to others?

Did you feel that others listened to you carefully enough?

Did you support others and build on their ideas?

Did you receive support from others, and did they build on your ideas?

What unconscious behavior may have helped or hindered your performance?

Attributes: Students are asked to go through the clothing section of the catalog and look for models who best exemplify their idea of the ideal man, woman, girl, and boy. They record in their journals what factors influenced their choices—e.g. physique, hair style and color, clothing style. They are then asked to consider the following question: To what extent is your concept of the ideal person influenced by catalog models and the like?

The ideal models chosen can be shared in small groups for comparison and discussion.

Missing Pages: Each student picks a page at random from the appliance section and considers how his life would be changed if these particular appliances did not exist.

Furniture: Each student furnishes his own imaginary living room from the pages of the catalog, listing and describing the items chosen in his journal. They then write brief answers to the following questions: How does this room reflect your personality? What does your selection say about you? Can you identify some of the influences which have led to your decisions?

The class breaks up into small groups and each person

shares his room with his group. The group discusses what image they think each room projects and compares these impressions with what the individual thinks his room projects about himself.

Automobiles: Students look through the automotive section of the catalog and select the items that appeal to them. They then decide which items are designed to improve the function of the car, and which are designed to enhance the self-image of the driver or owner. Discussion and journal writing consider what influences have caused the items to be appealing.

Toys: Each student selects three toys from the catalog which he would have liked but did not have at age seven. Lists can be collected and read anonymously in small groups, with group members guessing the author of each list.

Toys and Society: The group examines a page taken at random from the toy section of the catalog and discusses what aspects of our society and culture are reflected in the toys. If this discussion has taken place in small groups, each group can choose a representative to deliver an impromptu mini-lecture to the class, composed by the group as a whole.

Index: A piece of paper, or the blackboard, is divided down the middle; one side is marked "Necessities" and the other "Luxuries." One member of the group reads off a column picked at random from the Index of the catalog. The group decides by consensus whether each item should go on the "Necessities" or the "Luxuries" list. If this activity has been done in small groups, the groups can share their lists and discuss them.

JOURNAL-SYNTHESIZING ACTIVITIES

The following activities can be assigned to an entire class, to a small group, or to individuals after they have had sufficient experience writing in the journals. All of these activities may be profitably repeated after a suitable interval has elapsed.

Important Note:

These synthesizing activities are designed as private writing. They must not be used as composition topics in the conventional sense. As with all private writing, the student may share it if he chooses, of course.

If the teacher wishes to assign public writing based upon the contents of the journal, he must exercise great care in his selection of topics and he must make it absolutely clear to the students *in advance* that it is to be public writing. And, of course, he must respect the students' right to pass.

Time Capsule: Your journal is discovered one hundred years from now (or three hundred years ago). You, your other-time counterpart, find the journal. Write a description of the person and the way of life revealed in the journal.

Missing: You have been missing for three months. A member of the Missing Persons Bureau and your older brother, who hasn't seen you in ten years, are looking through your journal trying to reconstruct the kind of person you are. Write their conversation.

Parents: Imagine that your father (or mother) reads your journal. Record his (her) first reactions. Write five sentences.

Simile: List five adjectives that best characterize the

personality contained in your journal. Write a simile to illustrate each quality (e.g. cautious, like a night fighter crossing a mine field; boring, like a volunteer Santa at the orphanage Christmas party).

Interview: Select five pages from your journal that you might be willing to show to a college admissions officer. Write a profile of your personality based only on the contents of those five pages.

Found Poem: Search through your journal for apt phrases or interesting images. String these together to create a "found poem."

Wedding Party: Select four of your friends to serve as best man and ushers or maid-of-honor and bridesmaids at your wedding. Imagine that they read your journal just before your marriage. Compose a toast that each might give at the bridal dinner.

Doctors and Dentists: Think of a person who knows you in a limited way, such as your doctor or dentist. Suppose that person read your journal. Write down the five most important new things that that person might learn about you.

Enemies: Think of someone you know that you believe holds you in low esteem. Find five things in your journal that would help him to change his mind about you. Incorporate these into a letter which your best friend might write to this person.

Changes: Think of a person who knew you well at some time earlier in your life. What might that person say about how you have changed, based upon the evidence in the journal?

ART WORK IN ENGLISH CLASS

People experience strong emotional responses to color and line, responses which are frequently subconscious and unarticulated. Using color and line to represent an abstract concept, it is often possible to express feelings that one could not have expressed had he been limited to verbal communication. Further, in selecting and manipulating colors, a person may discover dimensions in his own responses that would otherwise have gone undetected. The physical manipulation of the materials may deepen one's self-understanding as well as one's understanding of the concept.

Materials required are the following: Assorted sheets of colored paper (8½ x 11), colored paper strips (½ x 2½), and glue or paste. It is important that there be an adequate supply of all available colors, and that the range of colors be as broad as possible.

To create a color/line representation, the student chooses one 8½x11-inch sheet to be his background, and glues the strips he chose to each other and to the background according to his own design. The strips need not all be attached to the background, but the finished work must be both attached and related to the background.

The following activities allow for a synthesis of verbal communication and esthetic response. Each activity can profitably be followed by group discussion and/or additional writing activities. However, it is important to keep in mind that students should not be pressured to explain the meaning of their collages or of any particular portion thereof. The right to pass must be gently but firmly upheld.

HOME AND WAR

1. Students write in their journals a sentence or two

in answer to the following questions:

> Identify a moment when you were really, really happy.
>
> What was the best meal you ever had? Who served it to you?
>
> What is something you made that you were really proud of?
>
> What is a present that someone gave you that you really enjoyed? Who gave it to you?
>
> Describe something that someone you love did that made you really glad.
>
> What toy that you owned gave you great pleasure?
>
> Of all the beds you have slept in, which was your favorite? Which brings back the fondest memories?
>
> Did you ever have a secret place? A hide-out? A hut? A place that was your own special place?
>
> What was the nicest gathering of people you remember?
>
> What thing would you like to show others that holds a piece of you?

2. Students list the *place* where each of these good memories originated, being as specific as possible.

3. Using all these good-memory-producing places as a starting point, each student tries to create in his imagination one place that would be perfect for him—his ideal place—his ideal home.

4. Each student then makes a color/line representation of his ideal place.

(Optional: To set the mood the teacher may play one of the following records:

"Homeward Bound"—Simon and Garfunkel
"Green, Green Grass of Home"—Curly Putnam
"Country Road"—James Taylor
"Penny Lane"—The Beatles

Or he might read James Wright's poem "The Blessing" and, perhaps, Robert Burns' "My Heart Is in the Highlands.")

5. When students have finished constructing their ideal place, the teacher asks them to make another color/line representation—this one to portray their concept of war.

ADDITIONAL ACTIVITIES

Each student can write a dialogue between his two creations.

The teacher can post all the war representations on one wall, all the ideal place representations on another wall. The class may discuss the qualities they see in each and the responses they evoke.

The teacher collects all the ideal place representations; then, one by one, rips them up. Each student writes a description of what his creation was and what it has now become. The teacher suggests that students might consider sending their descriptions with the ripped up pieces, to their Congressman or Senator, accompanied by a short letter urging him to work to prevent wars. (Teacher should provide addresses, envelopes, stationery, and stamps.)

THE POWER OF POSITIVE THINKING

A friend of ours, for years a great collector of phonograph records, recently sorted through his vast collection and selected the songs that have the most pleasant associations for him. From these records he has created one unbroken forty-five minute tape recording, with a clip from one record, a longer section from another, all arranged in a progression meaningful to him. From time to time he listens to the tape, recovering pleasant moments of his past, lifting his spirits, recharging his vitality.

Athletes sometimes use hypnosis or auto-hypnosis to improve their future performances by repeatedly visualizing success. Maxwell Maltz, in *Psychocybernetics,* urges essentially the same approach. Maltz defines worrying as negative goal setting; he suggests that visualizing images of failure will pull one towards failure just as surely as visualizing images of success will pull one toward success.

For this activity, the teacher gives the following instructions: Think for a moment about the next six months of your life. What are your plans, your hopes, your goals, your projects? What does this six-month period hold in store for you? How is it likely to turn out? When you are ready, make two color/line representations of this six-month period—one representing the worst possible outcome the period might have, the other representing the best possible outcome it could have.

When the constructions are completed, the teacher says: Take a close look at your art work, allowing yourself to fully experience your reactions. . . . Now destroy the representation of the worst possible outcome. Display your representation of the best possible outcome in a place where you will see it often, perhaps on your bedroom wall.

MOTHER, LOVE, SEX, WAR[2]

The teacher gives each student a paper with one of the above four words on it. No one knows anyone else's assignment. Each student makes a color/line representation of the concept assigned him. When he has finished, he hangs his creation on the wall.

When everyone's construction has been posted, the teacher tells the group, "The concepts represented are Mother, Love, Sex, and War. Would anyone care to tell what his creation means to him?" Some people will prefer to remain silent; others will be eager to explain their creations. Plenty of time must be allowed, but the teacher must also be sure to protect those who choose not to speak.

Next, students move their creations so that all representations of one concept are together, Mother on this wall, Love on that, Sex here, and War over there. Constructions can then be compared for similarities and differences, and for patterns. (Frequently—though not dependably—the sex/war creations use strong, bright colors—reds, blacks, oranges, yellows; the mother/love creations use pastels—light greens, soft pinks, lavenders, light blues.)

SATISFYING LEARNING

The teacher asks students to think back over their lives, reviewing learning experiences they have had that were really satisfying to them at the time they had them. He then asks them to list the nine most satisfying learning experiences they have ever had. The wording is important. To the question, "Do you mean in school?" the answer is, "That depends on you. List the nine learn-

---

2. Suggested by Prof. Nathaniel S. French.

ing experiences that were most satisfying to you."

Students then rank order these nine experiences according to the amount of satisfaction each afforded at the time they had the experience. The most satisfying is number one, the least number nine.

Next, each student creates a color/line representation of what constitutes a satisfying learning experience for him right now. When construction is completed, students discuss the meaning of their creations in groups of three or four.

Students may next create a color/line representation of "My School."

All the "My School" creations can be posted on one wall, and all the "Satisfying Learning" compositions on another. Examine for similarities and differences. Discussion might focus on specific ways to incorporate some of the colors and lines of the "Satisfying Learning" group into the "My School" creations. This could lead to the writing of a group proposal which might be sent to the principal.

Each student can write a dialogue between his two creations.

Each student can make a list of five specific things he can do to make school a more satisfying learning experience for him. Groups of four or five people then share their lists, and in turn make one list of five things that the group might do together, or for each other, to make school a more satisfying learning experience. These lists should then be shared with the entire class. Some people may wish to draft self-contracts.

Students can write descriptions of their creations for "My School" and "Satisfying Learning." The creations and descriptions can be sent to the principal, or to a parent, or to the Superintendent of Schools, or the local school committee, or the local newspaper. Or several of them can be put together to make up a display for the next meeting of the P.T.A.

INFLUENTIAL PEOPLE

The teacher gives directions as follows:

1. Divide your life in two halves. Think about all the people who have had a strong influence on you. List four people from the early half of your life, and four from the second half.

2. Now list four people who still have a strong influence on you right now.

3. Place a check mark beside the name of each person whose influence you feel was or is good.

4. Select one of the people whose name you have checked and make a color/line representation of the influence he has had on you.

5. Write a description of your creation. Consider writing this person a note of thanks, and sending it—along with your creation and description—to him. Most probably he is preoccupied with his own self-doubts and has forgotten the lift he gave you. Perhaps being reminded will give him a lift.

THIS CLASSROOM

The teacher asks the students to think about their present class for a few moments, considering such questions as: Who talks frequently? Who talks most? Who is generally silent? What groups have influence? On whom? How important is the teacher? How much does he talk? What kind of influence does he exert? What is the atmosphere like (warm, exciting, frightening, boring, etc.)? Is the atmosphere the same in all parts of the room? What emotions prevail in this room? What part do you play in this class? What has your participation been like? What have your rewards been?

When they are ready, students make color/line representations of "This Classroom." As each student finishes his creation, he writes a description of it and gives both the description and the creation to the teacher. If he wishes, he may include some suggestions about how the classroom could be made a better place for him.

Sub-selves: The process of decision-making can be analyzed as the outcome of an argument between sub-selves of one personality. For this activity, the student can think of a particular decision he has made recently, or the teacher can pose a problem (e.g. Should I tell the truth about why I don't want to go to _____.'s party or make up an excuse?) The students think about at least three sub-selves that participate in their decision. A color/line representation can then be made of what went into that decision.

Lists: A color/line representation may be made to symbolize any of the following lists: Your ten happiest moments. Five things you have done that you are really proud of. Twenty things you really love to do. The ten most exciting moments in your life. The ten achievements you are most proud of. The ten successes that mean the most to you. The two lists in a Force-Field Analysis.

Objects of Love: Students think about someone or something they have loved or love now and compose a color/line representation of their relationship. They may choose:

a) An object that you really love(d).

b) A person of an older generation whom you really love(d).

c) A person of a younger generation whom you really love(d).

d) A contemporary of the same sex whom you really love(d).

e) A contemporary of the opposite sex whom you really love(d).

f) A pet that you really love(d).

LETTER WRITING WITH A POSITIVE FOCUS

One of the tasks of a teacher of composition is to provide each student with writing opportunities which involve genuine and significant communication and which the student sees as worthwhile. Letter writing can be such an activity if it is not conducted along traditional lines (i.e. make-believe business letters). Letter writing may be scheduled on a regular basis or it may be spontaneous. Letters should always be addressed to real people and should actually be mailed. If possible, the school should provide stationery, envelopes, stamps, postcards, and a convenient mailbox.

Many students will need no prompting from the teacher and will welcome the chance to use class time to write some letters they have been wanting to write. Others may profit from some pump priming. The following are some sample primers:

1. Do you remember the person who ran along behind you when you were learning how to ride

GENERAL TECHNIQUES AND ACTIVITIES [153

a bicycle, the person who held you up when you were learning to swim, the person who put on your snowsuit, who helped you snap your galoshes, who taught you how to tie a bow? Consider sending each a thank-you postcard.

2. Is there anyone in your life who is helping you snap your metaphorical galoshes? List some things that person has done for you in the last two years. Consider writing and telling him.

3. Think of five gifts you have received—ones you really enjoy. Consider sending an additional note of thanks.

4. Think of three non-famous people you admire greatly. For each person list three qualities you particularly admire. Consider sending postcards or letters.

5. Think of a specific incident in which you were aided by someone, someone who might even be unaware he had helped. Describe the incident. Say thanks.

6. List some things you have done this year that you are proud of. Think of a person who at one time was interested in your life but who has been out of touch with you recently. Write this person and bring him up to date. Use your list.

7. Select a person you like or admire or appreciate

or love. Apply the *Brivihafo Positive Feedback Generator*:[3]

Pick *at random* one word from each of the six columns. Try to think of a specific incident or incidents in which the person you selected exhibited the characteristics you chose. Write the person a letter and tell him.

The principle of random choosing can be applied

\multicolumn{3}{c}{**BRIVIHAFO POSITIVE FEEDBACK GENERATOR**}
I	**II**	**III**
1. supportive	1. reassuring	1. zestful
2. kind	2. encouraging	2. helpful
3. attentive	3. dependable	3. accepting
4. cooperative	4. loyal	4. refreshing
5. stimulating	5. thoughtful	5. inclusive
6. enthusiastic	6. considerate	6. thorough
7. trustworthy	7. influential	7. valuable
8. perceptive	8. affectionate	8. sensitive
9. wise	9. vital	9. ardent
10. warm	10. tactful	10. creative
IV	**V**	**VI**
1. tender	1. honest	1. neat
2. responsible	2. trusting	2. cool
3. alive	3. friendly	3. delightful
4. steadfast	4. right on	4. empathetic
5. forthright	5. deferential	5. inspiring
6. reasonable	6. positive	6. zealous
7. loving	7. arousing	7. clever
8. insightful	8. useful	8. reliable
9. energetic	9. sympathetic	9. open
10. uplifting	10. aware	10. astute

3. The Brivihafo Positive Feedback Generator is named for its originators—David Britton, Michael Vitiello, Robert Hawley, and John Foss.

cynically or seriously, and in addition to being used as a thank-you note generator, random choice lists such as the Brivihafo can easily be invented to fill such other uses as a small-talk generator, a what's-wrong-with-the-world generator.

8. List the four most interesting things that have happened to you in school this year. Think of a teacher who has taken a special interest in you or who has meant something to you in this or earlier years. Bring him up to date.

9. List three people with whom you are in emphatic agreement about something. Write and tell them. And if you are willing to *do* anything to support them, tell them that too.

10. List three people who have worked hard on specific tasks. Tell them you noticed their effort.

11. List three people who have done things you approve of. Tell them.

12. Imagine that you and your parents will never see or hear from each other again. Bring the record up to date; tell your parents what they have meant to you.

13. Celebrities receive loads of fan letters; politicians receive piles of letters, also. Select a less prominent person in the news, one who pleases you for some reason. Tell him. It will give him a lift. Maybe he will answer.

14. Look at the section of the newspaper entitled "Letters to the Editor." Select a letter you agree with. The author is probably desperate to know how people have received his message. Tell him. Be sure to include a return address—maybe he will answer.

15. The amount of junk mail carried by the postman is staggering in quantity and, for the most part, repulsive in quality. Choose an address at random out of the phone book and write a "junk" letter addressed to "Occupant." See if you can improve on the quality of the usual junk mail. Be sure to include a return address, and see if you can inspire "Occupant" to reply.

16. The teacher posts a master list of the students' names, addresses, and birthdays. The students are encouraged to write letters to one another. If a student receives a letter, he must write an answer.

17. Each week the teacher posts a list of people who could use a lift, with names, ages, addresses, and circumstances. Likely sources include orphanages, prisons, veterans' hospitals, children's hospitals, old people's homes, the Red Cross for disaster victims, newspaper items. Gradually students will add to the lists themselves. The list should be brought up to date each week.

18. The teacher posts a list of people who have done things worthy of praise, with names, ages, ad-

dresses, and circumstances. Likely sources of information include student activities, local churches, clubs, other teachers, police, social workers, etc. Bring list up to date each week.

19. The teacher contacts another teacher from a different part of the town or another state or country to set up pen pal correspondences.

20. Set up a "Dear Abby" clinic. A letter from an anonymous student is posted and students respond with sympathy or advice—if they wish. Teacher forwards the replies.

TABLE VII	
Critical Thinking Skills Fostered by the Personal Growth Approach to Composition	
Observing:	The pattern of wind in a puddle; a TV announcer with the sound off; how others react to your new clothes.
Comparing:	Food prices in suburbs and ghetto; the philosophy of your school and its rules; your and other people's reaction to a news item.
Classifying:	Colleges; ways of spending Sunday afternoons; things you love to do.
Reporting:	Events at a football game; impressions of a trip to a foreign neighborhood; feelings of joy, anger, pity.

(continued on following page)

TABLE VII

Critical Thinking Skills Fostered by the Personal Growth Approach to Composition

Discovering:	How to adjust a carburetor; why teenagers smoke; a new way to deal with your sister.
Evaluating:	Newspaper columnists; teachers' comments about your work; a friend's praise.
Summarizing:	The Israeli position in the Mid-East; the best things about school; your goals and aspirations five, ten, fifteen years ahead.
Analyzing Data:	The "facts" on drugs; the positions of ten friends on smoking; your rank orders.
Creating:	A new song; a way to evaluate students without marks; a new way to learn about yourself.
Criticizing:	The way textbooks deal with black history; the latest imitation rock group; the draft system.
Checking Assumptions:	Behind the grading system; behind the involvement in Southeast Asia; behind your self-image.
Defining Words:	Such as "radical," "peace with honor," "hero," "under-achiever," "teaching," "learning," "lazy."

8

Ongoing Activities

SOME ACTIVITIES DESIGNED to stimulate oral and written discussions are best executed only once. Other activities are most rewarding when conducted on a regular basis. The following is a listing of activities which can be scheduled on a more or less regular basis, perhaps at the same time once or twice each week.

Many people draw comfort from tradition, from ritual, from the repetition of familiar and predictable patterns. Once a pattern of scheduling for these ongoing activities has been established, it is wise to adhere to it unless compelling reasons intervene.

THOUGHT CARDS

Once a week (usually on the same day each week) each student turns in a 4" x 6" card on which he has recorded an observation, an epigram, a problem, a statement, a poem, or any other notation. The teacher selects a few of these cards to read to the class, concealing the author's identity. Or the teacher may begin by reading three cards chosen at random on the first day, and a few more on successive days. The class is given time to respond to the selections read.

At the end of six weeks or so, the teacher may return the cards to the students. They may then write "I Learned..." statements in their journals.

Or the teacher may distribute ditto masters and ask

each student (or volunteers) to contribute one or more of their thoughts to a class magazine. Or, concealing the names, the teacher might distribute each stack of thought cards to someone other than the writer. The reader would record his reactions in the form of another thought card, an essay, or a dramatic monologue, and turn this in to the teacher, who conveys the cards and response to the original author.

We have found students to be enthusiastic about writing thought cards when they feel that their cards have a good chance of being read and responded to by the teacher and other students. We have also found it advisable that the teacher refrain from commenting on spelling, grammar, or rhetorical style except when specifically and privately asked to do so by the author.

WEEKLY REACTION SHEETS

Once a week students are given time to fill out a Weekly Reaction Sheet which they put in their journals. At the end of two months, the students are asked to set out their Weekly Reaction Sheets side-by-side, in chronological order, and to examine their answers to each question, looking for patterns. The teacher may then call for some "I Learned . . ." statements, or for a special Telegram to Myself.

Two examples of Weekly Reaction Sheets follow.

WEEKLY REACTION SHEET I

Week of _____ to _____

1. List ten things you did last week that you feel good about:

    1. _____
    2. _____
    3. _____
    4. _____
    5. _____
    6. _____
    7. _____
    8. _____
    9. _____
    10. _____

2. Identify a situation or person who threatened you. How did you react?

3. What did you procrastinate about last week?

4. Identify three choices you made last week:

    1. _____
    2. _____
    3. _____

(continued on following page)

WEEKLY REACTION SHEET I

5. List three people who did things that made you feel good. What did each do?

   1. _____
   2. _____
   3. _____

6. Were you in strong disagreement with anyone this week? How did you handle it?

WEEKLY REACTION SHEET II

Name _____ Week beginning _____, ending _____

1. What was the high point of your week?
2. Did you initiate any changes in your life this week?
3. How could the week have been better?
4. Did you make any plans this week for some future event?
5. Open comment:

TELEGRAM TO MYSELF

Once a week each student is asked to write a telegram to himself. The telegram should contain a message of importance—an announcement of an unusual event, an unusual observation, a reminder to do something. Students should try to limit their messages to eleven words to avoid overcharges. "Love" is free. The telegrams should be kept in the students' journals, and at the end of some time, such as eight weeks, each student should reread his stack of telegrams, providing answers where indicated.

LETTER TO THE TEACHER

Once a week each student is asked to write a private letter to the teacher. The teacher stores these letters in individual folders, one for each student, in a locked box. The teacher reads the letters privately and writes his responses at the bottom of each letter. The folders are returned to the students so they can read the teacher's answers, and then collected and locked away until the next letter-writing day.

PUBLIC LETTERS

Writing letters-to-the-editor, letters to congressmen, the mayor, the President, company executives, the superintendent of schools, authors, etc., is one way of moving values into action by public affirmation. A time should be set aside each week for public letter writing, and the teacher should supply stationery, stamps, and a list of addresses. Letters should be short and to the point and should avoid defamatory statements. Some students may wish to post copies of their letters on the bulletin board. Copies or first drafts of letters can be kept in the journal, along with any answers that are received.

BULLETIN BOARDS

The bulletin board should provide a constantly changing source of stimulation for conversation and writing. The photo-of-the-week, cartoon-of-the-week, quote-of-the-week, advertisement-of-the-week, collage-of-the-week, joke-of-the-week could be brought in by students on a rotating basis, or entries could be submitted to a bulletin board committee. If the class is not too large, each member of the class can be given a space to use as he wants. With a larger class, students can have turns, keeping spaces for perhaps three weeks at a stretch. One section of the board can serve as the class newspaper, with a variety of articles, columns, and stories which may be changed weekly.

MINUTE DIARY

Each student is asked to pick one minute of his day, say 5:37 to 5:38 P.M. He is asked to make note of his activities, thoughts, and feelings in that minute and record them in his journal in class the next day. After there have been many such entries, they are compared for patterns.

HOUR DIARY

Each student is asked to pick one hour of his week, say 1 P.M. to 2 P.M. on Fridays. His activities, thoughts, and feelings during that hour are entered in his journal each week. After a certain number of weeks, the entries may be compared for patterns.

UNFINISHED BUSINESS

A valuable routine is the setting aside of a period of time each week for unfinished business. The students can use this time to complete conversations that they started earlier, to finish letters, to search their journals, or to reflect on the events of the week. In order to achieve a productive atmosphere, it is important that the time set aside for unfinished business be inviolate, never preempted by other exigencies however pressing.

9

Personal-Growth Activities for Teachers

IF YOU ARE NEW to the theory and techniques of *Composition for Personal Growth*, you will undoubtedly encounter questions and problems as you use this approach. Many of your difficulties you will resolve with experience and time. However, it is very helpful to confer with colleagues in your own, or a neighboring school, who may also be embarking on this innovative program. If you can, it is advisable to meet together on some sort of regular basis for mutual help and support.

We have included here some activities that you can do together to clarify your goals and techniques in using *Composition for Personal Growth*. The activities suggested here are most fruitful when done together by a group. But, if you do not have contact with others who are also using this approach, you can adapt these activities for your own individual use. Think about them, respond to them, or just read them. You will probably find them thought-provoking and helpful.

SITUATIONS AND ALTERNATIVES

For each situation below, circle the response you think is best; mark with an X the one you consider worst. If you are not altogether satisfied with the response you circled, compose another option. Discuss each situation with colleagues.

1. You have just read aloud the third of five Thought Cards. Discussion has followed the reading of the first two. As you finish reading the third, one of your students says, "Boy, another phony card; I think this whole business is silly." What do you do?

    a. Point out that comments should try to be constructive, and inform the student that you would be glad to discuss the worth of the activity at another time.

    b. Say nothing, and if no additional comment is offered, continue with the cards.

    c. Ask him what he means by "phony."

    d. Acknowledge that everyone is entitled to his opinion. Invite others to comment on the student's statement.

    e.

2. You have just given instructions for an activity for the whole class to participate in. The class appears eager to begin. You ask for last minute questions. Johnny says, "I enjoy these games as much as anyone, but I'm beginning to worry about whether I'll know enough English to survive in Miss X's class next term." What do you say?

    a. Don't worry. You'll know enough English and a lot more besides. Let's get on with the activity.

b. Class, you have participated in activities like this on other occasions. I would like you to make a list of all the things you think you might learn from this activity. Then check any item on your list which might be particularly applicable to Johnny's concern.

c. Relax, Johnny; just because you're having fun doesn't mean you're not learning anything. Let's talk later on.

d. Johnny, the research that's been done on this program indicates that students who have participated in it write just as well as, or better than, students who've had a traditional English composition program.

e.

3. You have just distributed a questionnaire to be filled out anonymously. You explain that a chart of all responses will be handed out the next day. Linda says, "I don't care how others respond. And I already know what I think. I don't see why I have to do this." How do you reply?

   a. Would you question any assignment you received—for example, 'read pages 202-218 in your text'—or do you reserve your skepticism for things that aren't supported by tradition?

   b. A pass is always a legitimate response. You needn't participate.

c. Others may be interested in how *you* respond. If you fill out the questionnaire, you needn't feel obligated to read how others responded.

d. Since you are so different from the others in not caring what your peers think, it might be interesting to see if you are equally different in your responses to the items on the questionnaire. I'll bet you'd find the comparison instructive. Why don't you try it?

e.

MY DAY IN COURT
1. Brainstorm possible responses to each of the following charges:

   a. You are accused of amateur psychologizing. As a teacher unqualified to meddle with the adolescent psyche, your assignments are reckless.

   b. You are charged with using the young as guinea pigs for inadequately tested and potentially dangerous materials.

   c. You are accused of using English class for fun and games.

   d. You are poking into the private affairs of the young—into areas heretofore reserved for the family and/or the church.

   e. You are undermining real education by giving the young the impression that the titilation of some superficial psychological tactics is as worthy as the enduring satisfaction afforded by the mastery of an academic discipline.

    f. You are encouraging intensive self-examination in an age group already nearly paralyzed by self-consciousness and self-doubt.

2. Role Play: You are summoned to court to answer one of the six charges listed above. You are questioned by one of the groups listed below.

    a. Three traditional teachers (good ones) who are scandalized by your program.

    b. Three parents who have asked for a conference.

    c. The principal, assistant principal, and English department chairman (until now a supporter of experimentation).

3. List additional charges that one might encounter as a result of using these materials, and brainstorm appropriate defenses.

TEACHER SELF-EVALUATION

Although it would be difficult, and indeed obsessive, to conduct a formal evaluation of every class, it is important that the teacher form the habit of informally reviewing each class session and considering which activities were successful and which need to be revised or discarded. Aspects to be considered include appropriateness of time allowances, whether the students (and the teacher) *enjoyed* the class, what follow-up, if any, is needed, how the experience could be improved. Many teachers find it useful to record their self-evaluations. The following form is suggested for this purpose.

TEACHER'S SELF-EVALUATION

1. Did the students enjoy the class?
2. Was there adequate time for the activities?
3. Did the activities produce good discussion?
4. Was there time for writing?
5. Was there time for reflection?
6. Was the class sufficiently orderly and purposeful?
7. How can the class best follow up on these activities?
8. Was there serendipity or whimsy present in this class?
9. Was there a chance for student initiative?
10. Did the activities accomplish the objectives set forth in the lesson plan?
11. How can I use the students' responses in my future planning?
12. General comments:

— Were skills of spelling, grammar, composition used or tested?

Suggested Readings

Psychology

Maslow, Abraham H. *Motivation and Personality*, 2nd Edition. New York: Harper & Row, 1970.

Murray, Henry A. *Explorations in Personality*. New York: Science Editions, 1968.

Perls, F. S., Hefferline, R. F., and Goodman, P. *Gestalt Therapy: Excitement and Growth in Human Personality*. New York: Dell Books, 1965.

Perls, Frederick S. *Gestalt Therapy Verbatim*. Lafayette, California: Real People Press (P. O. Box 542), 1969.

Creative Problem Solving

Gordon, W. J. J. *The Metaphorical Way of Learning and Knowing*. Cambridge, Mass.: Porpoise Books, 1971.

Parnes, S. J. *Creative Behavior Guidebook*. New York: Charles Scribner's Sons, 1967.

Prince, G. M. *The Practice of Creativity: A Manual For Dynamic Group Problem Solving*. Evanston, Illinois: Harper and Row, 1970.

Values

Raths, L., Harmin, M., and Simon, S. B. *Values and Teaching: Working with Values in the Classroom*. Columbus, Ohio: Charles E. Merrill Publishing Co., 1966.

Simon, Sidney, Howe, Leland, and Kirschenbaum, Howard. *Values Clarification: A Handbook Practical of Strategies*. New York: Hart Publishing Co., 1972.

Handbooks of Activities:

Hawley, Robert C., and Hawley, Isabel L. *A Handbook of*

Personal Growth Activities for Classroom Use. Amherst, Mass.: Education Research Associates (P. O. Box 767), 1972.

Malamud, D. I., and Machover, S. *Toward Self Understanding: Group Techniques in Self-Confrontation.* Springfield, Ill.: Charles C. Thomas, 1965.

Pfeiffer, J. William, and Jones, John E. *A Handbook of Structured Experiences for Human Relations Training* (3 vols.). Iowa City, Iowa: University Associates Press, 1971.

English Teaching

Dixon, John. *Growth Through English.* Reading, England: National Association for the Teaching of English, 1967.

Moffett, James. *Teaching the Universe of Discourse.* Boston: Houghton Mifflin Company, 1968.

Muller, Herbert J. *The Uses of English.* New York: Holt, Rinehart, and Winston, 1967.

Skills for English Teachers

Semantics:

Hayakawa, S. I. *Language in Thought and Action,* 2nd edition. New York: Harcourt, Brace and World, Inc., 1964.

Postman, Neil, and Weingartner, Charles. *Teaching as a Subversive Activity.* New York: Delacorte Press, 1969.

Rhetoric:

Gibson, Walker. *Tough, Sweet, and Stuffy: An Essay on Modern American Prose Styles.* Bloomington, Ind.: Indiana University Press, 1970.

Usage:

Strunk, William, Jr., and White, E. B. *The Elements of Style.* New York: Macmillan Company, 1959.

Transformational Grammar:

Cattell, N. R. *The New English Grammar: A Descriptive Introduction.* Cambridge, Mass.: MIT Press, 1969.

Theatre:

Pemberton, R. N., Billing, N., and Clegg, J. D. *Teaching*

Drama. London: University of London Unibooks, 1972.

Spolin, Viola. *Improvisation for the Theater: A Handbook of Teaching and Directing Techniques.* Evanston, Ill.: Northwestern University Press, 1963.

Poetry Writing:
Koch, Kenneth. *Wishes, Lies, and Dreams: Teaching Children to Write Poetry.* New York: Random House, 1971.

English Composition

Christensen, Francis. *The Christensen Rhetoric Program: Teacher's Manual.* Evanston, Ill.: Harper and Row, 1968.

Leavitt, H. D. and Sohn, D. A. *Stop, Look, and Write!* New York: Bantam Books, 1964.

Moffett, James. *A Student-Centered Language Arts Curriculum, Grades K-13: A Handbook for Teachers.* Boston: Houghton Mifflin Company, 1968.

Research in Composition

Braddock, Richard, Lloyd-Jones, Richard, and Schoer, Lowell. *Research in Written Composition.* Champaign, Ill.: National Council of Teachers of English (508 South Sixth St.), 1963.

Britton, David D. *Composition for Personal Growth: Teacher Preparation and Evaluation.* Unpublished dissertation, University of Massachusetts, Amherst, 1972.

Hawley, Robert C. *Composition for Personal Growth: Program Design and Evaluation.* Unpublished dissertation, University of Massachusetts, Amherst, 1972.

Tovatt, Anthony, et al. *A Sampler of Practices in Teaching Junior and Senior High School English.* Muncie, Ind.: Ball State University, 1965.

Research in Group Processes

Luft, Joseph, *Group Processes: An Introduction to Group Dynamics,* 2nd edition. Palo Alto, California: National Press Books, 1970.

Schmuck, Richard A., and Schmuck, Patricia A. *Group Processes in the Classroom*. Dubuque, Iowa: Wm. C. Brown Company, 1971.

Grades and Grading

Kirschenbaum, Howard, Simon, Sidney B., and Napier, Rodney W. *Wad-Ja-Get? The Grading Game in American Education*. New York: Hart Publishing Company, 1971.

INDEX

INDEX

Acceptance and rejection. *See* interpersonal relations.
accomplishments, 52-54
acknowledgement, 90
action testing, 129-130
activities, 19, 26-61, 64-67, 72-73, 83-85, 89, 118-119, 125-130, 142-164, 166-170
   accomplishments, 52-54
   anger, 30
   arm and hand, 55-56
   arm drop, 50
   blindfolded conversation, 56-57
   body changes, 56
   brainstorming, 72
   card-sort center, 29
   "clay" sculpture, 64-65
   coat of arms, 57-58
   commandments, 46-49
   defining success, 31-35
   emotion list, 31
   family sayings, 42
   five things that make you feel good, 28
   guessing each other's behavior, 66
   Have you noticed?, 50-52

home and war, 144-146
homonyms, 30
"I am" statements, 43
"I believe" statements, 129-130
"I learned" statements, 128-129, 130
identity areas, 26-27
identity influences, 44-46
influential people, 150
inventing stories, 28
learning experiences, 35-38
lemons, 55
letter writing, 152-157
magazine stereotypes, 42
magic box, 28
moments, 40-41
mother, love, sex, war, 148
motivation, 19
offspring, aged sixteen, 55
paper tower, 66-67
positive thinking, 146-147
postcards, 73
preferences, 38-40
public affirmation, 72
satisfying experiences, 59-61

satisfying learning, 148-150
secrets, 49-50
strength bombardment, 65-66
talking with parents, 42
telegram, 72
this classroom, 150-151
What am I good at?, 52
Who am I?, 30
   See also activity groups, identity, inter personal relations, journal-synthesizing, letter writing, rank-order problems, topical inventories, values into action.
activity groups, 86-89
address lists, 84
advice, teaching, 97-103
alternatives search, 110-111
analysis
   spectrum, 110
   force-field, 112-113
anger, 30
approach. *See* teaching personal growth approach.
aptitude. *See* What am I good at?
arm and hand, 55-56
arm drop, 50
art in classroom, 144
assignments. *See* activities, activity groups.
attitude, student, 83. *See also* troubleshooting.
awareness
   and growth, 78-79
   body, 54-57
   class-meeting, 89. *See also* listening skills, personal growth.

Behavior, classroom, 62-63, 93-96
biography, 133
blindfolded conversation, 56-57
body
   awareness, 54-57
   changes, 56
   identity, 54
brainstorming, 72, 109-110
Brivihafo Positive Feedback Generator, 154-157
bulletin boards, 164

Card-sort center, 29
catalog buying, 137-141
caveats, 97-100
clarifying responses, 92
class activities. *See* activities, activity groups, groups.
class meetings, 85-86, 89. *See*

INDEX [181]

also fishbowling.
classroom
  behavior, 93-96
  effect of, 150-152
  "clay" sculpture, 64-65
  coat of arms, 57-58
  color-line representation, 148-151. *See also* art in classroom.
commandments, 46-49
competence determining, 49-54
competencies. *See* identity.
composition, purpose and procedures, 14-15, 19, 20, 21
"composition for personal growth" approach, 82-83, 85
confidence, 27
continuums, 123-124

Development reflection patterns, 91-93. *See also* personal growth.
diaries, 164
discipline. *See* troubleshooting.
discussion, 76-78
dynamics. *See* interpersonal relations.

Emotion list, 31. *See also* moments.
experience preferences, 38-40

Family sayings, 42
fantasy, 135-137
feedback, 75, 106-107. *See also* learning satisfaction, personal growth.
fishbowling, 89, 139-140
five things that make you feel good, 28
Flanders Interaction Analysis, 77
force-field analysis, 112-113
Fordham, Frieda, 12
four-corner game, 125-128
fundamental dynamics. *See* interpersonal relations.

Groups, 86-89, 96-97. *See also* activity groups.
growth, 76-79. *See also* personal growth.
guessing each other's behavior, 66

Have you noticed?, 50-52
home and war, 144-146
homonyms, 30

inventories.
journal-synthesizing activities, 142-143
Jung, C.G., 12

"I am" statements, 43
"I believe" statements, 129-130
"I learned" statements, 128-129, 130
identity
    activities, 28-35, 42-57
    areas of, 26-27
    body, 54-57
    competencies, 49-54
    formation, 22
    general, 57-61
    influences, 41-49
influences, external, 150
inventing stories, 28
inventories, 131-134
interpersonal relations, 62-68

Learning
    by doing, 75
    experiences, 35-38
    satisfaction, 148-149
lemons, 55
lesson plans, 104-105
let's hear from the others, 91
letter writing, 72, 152-158. *See also* Brivihafo Positive Feedback Generator, public affirmation.
Likert scale, 124
listening skills, 89-90

Jo-Hari model of awareness, 23-24
journals, 16. *See also* here-and-now, then-and-there words, home and war,

Magazine stereotypes, 42
magic box, 28
metaphor, 12
Meyer, Peter, 11-12
mnemonic device, 84
moments, 40-41
mother, love, sex, war, 148
motivation, 19

Name tags, 83-84

Observation questionnaire, 51
observers, process, 89, 90
offspring, aged sixteen, 55

Paper tower, 66-67
parents, talking with, 42
participation, 85-86, 91
percentage problems, 124-125
personal-growth approach, 15-16, 75-79
physical awareness, 54-57
pitfalls, teaching, 97-100
positive thinking, 146-147
postcards, 73
preferences, 38-40
priorities. *See* rank-order problems.
problem drama, 121
process observers, 89, 90
public affirmation, 72

Rank-order problems, 118-119. *See also* four-corner game.
rank-ordering teacher goals, 20
reaction sheet, weekly, 160-162
reflection patterns, 91-93
reinforcement. *See* support groups.
response, clarifying, 92
revealed differences survey, 122-123
role play, 116-122. *See also* journal-synthesizing activities, then-and-there words.

Satisfying experiences, 59-61
satisfying learning, 148-150
scale, Likert, 124
secrets, 49-50
self-confidence, 27
self-contracting, 111
self-evaluation, 71-72, 170-171. *See also* biography, reflection patterns, statements.
self-expression. *See* art in classroom.
self, three rings of, 25
singing Sam, 84-85

spectrum analysis, 110
statements
   "I am," 43
   "I believe," 129-130
   "I learned," 128-129, 130
stereotypes, 42
stories, inventing, 28
street theater, 121-122
strength bombardment, 65-66
student
   attitudes, 83, 150-152
   feedback, 106-108
success, 31-35
support groups, 96-97
survey, revealed differences, 122-123

objectives, 104
pitfalls, 97-100
See also troubleshooting.
technical skills, 103
telegram, 72-73
testing action, 129-130
then-and-there words, 130-131
thinking skills, 157-158
think tank, 91-92
this classroom, 150-151
thought cards, 159-160
three rings of self, 25
topical inventories, 134-141
troubleshooting, 93-96

Talking with parents, 42
task force, 80-82, 86
teacher
   activities, 166-169
   feedback, 107
   goals, 20
   procedures, 85
   responsibilities, 17-18
   role, 80-82
   self-evaluation, 166-171
   situations, 166-169
   skills, 103
teaching
   evaluation, 106
   lesson plans, 105
   methods, 86-89

Value free education, 73-74
values into action, 70-73

What am I good at?, 52
Who am I?, 30
Who wrote which stories?, 65
word games, 130-131
writing, 13-14. *See also* composition, inventories, journals, letter writing.

Notes